COGNITI   ΧΑΡΥ

In the last three decades cognitive behaviour therapy (CBT) has been applied to an ever-increasing number of problems (including anxiety disorders, substance abuse and eating disorders) and populations (children, adolescents and older people). The National Institute for Health and Care Excellence (NICE) recommends CBT as the first line treatment in the NHS for tackling a wide range of psychological disorders.

Cognitive Behaviour Therapy: 100 Key Points and Techniques is a crisp, concise elaboration of the 100 main features of this very popular and evidence-based approach within the field of psychotherapy. The 100 key points and techniques cover CBT theory as well as practice. Divided into helpful sections, topics covered include:

- misconceptions about CBT
- teaching the cognitive model
- assessment and case conceptualization
- homework (self-help assignments)
- ways of detecting and answering negative automatic thoughts (NATs)
- behavioural experiments
- intermediate and core beliefs
- relapse management
- third wave CBT.

For the second edition of this book, Michael Neenan and Windy Dryden have revised and updated many of the points and several new ones have been added. This neat, usable book is an essential guide for psychotherapists and counsellors, both trainee and qualified, who need to ensure they are entirely familiar with the key features of CBT as part of a general introduction to the current major psychotherapies.

Michael Neenan is Associate Director of the Centre for Stress Management and Centre for Coaching, Blackheath, and a BABCP accredited cognitive behavioural therapist. He has written and edited over 20 books.

Windy Dryden is Professor of Psychotherapeutic Studies at Goldsmiths College, University of London and is an international authority on rational emotive behaviour therapy (REBT). He has worked in psychotherapy for more than 30 years and is the author and editor of over 200 books.

100 Key Points and Techniques
Series Editor: Windy Dryden

ALSO IN THIS SERIES:

COGNITIVE BEHAVIOUR THERAPY

100 KEY POINTS AND TECHNIQUES

SECOND EDITION

michael neenan and windy dryden

Routledge
Taylor & Francis Group

LONDON AND NEW YORK

Second edition published 2015
by Routledge
27 Church Road, Hove, East Sussex, BN3 2FA

and by Routledge
711 Third Avenue, New York, NY 10017

Routledge is an imprint of the Taylor & Francis Group, an informa business

First edition published by Brunner-Routledge 2004

British Library Cataloguing in Publication Data
A catalogue record for this book is available from the
British Library

Library of Congress Cataloging in Publication Data
Neenan, Michael.
Cognitive behaviour therapy : 100 key points and techniques / Michael
Neenan and Windy Dryden. – Second edition.
pages cm
Includes bibliographical references.
ISBN 978-0-415-74335-8 (hardback) – ISBN 978-0-415-74336-5 (pbk.) –
ISBN 978-1-315-76247-0 (ebook) 1. Cognitive therapy. I. Dryden, Windy.
II. Title.
RC489.C63N45 2014
616.89′1425–dc23
2014004355

ISBN: 978-0-415-74335-8 (hbk)
ISBN: 978-0-415-74336-5 (pbk)
ISBN: 978-1-315-76247-0 (ebk)

Typeset in Aldus LT Std
by Saxon Graphics Ltd, Derby

Printed and bound by CPI Group (UK) Ltd,
Croydon, CR0 4YY

To Laurence for his steadfast support and loyalty
— M. N.

CONTENTS

Part 3
CBT PRACTICE

Getting started

Ways of detecting NATs

Examining and responding to NATs

Homework

Ways of identifying underlying assumptions and rules

Revising assumptions and rules

Uncovering core beliefs

Developing and strengthening new/existing core beliefs

Towards termination and beyond

CBT: is it just for clients?

Other issues

PREFACE

Cognitive behaviour therapy (CBT) is an umbrella term that covers a number of approaches such as rational emotive behaviour therapy, problem-solving training, cognitive therapy, metacognitive therapy, acceptance and commitment therapy, dialectical behaviour therapy, and mindfulness-based cognitive therapy. These approaches differ in the varying emphasis they place on cognitive versus behavioural principles and techniques but they all seek 'to replace maladaptive behaviors, emotions, and cognitions with more adaptive ones' (Craske, 2010: 4). The dominant model in the field of CBT is cognitive therapy (CT) that was developed by Aaron T. Beck (b. 1921), an American psychiatrist, at the University of Pennsylvania in the early 1960s. Beck's model is the main focus of this book and his institute in Philadelphia has changed its name from CT to CBT to reflect the fact that 'CT is often discussed under the generic label … CBT' (Beck and Dozois, 2011).

Beck's approach initially focused on research into and the treatment of depression (Beck et al., 1979), but in the last three decades CBT has been applied to an ever-increasing number of areas including anxiety disorders (Clark and Beck, 2010), substance abuse (Beck et al., 1993), personality disorders (Davidson, 2008), psychosis (Morrison, 2001), bipolar disorder (Newman et al., 2002), chronic medical problems (White, 2001), eating disorders (Fairburn, 2008), children, young people and families (Fuggle et al., 2013), and older people (James, 2010). Despite the ever-growing applications and seeming complexity of CBT, 'the cornerstone of cognitive theory and therapy of emotional disorders' is captured in the 'simple statement: "The way you think affects the way you feel".' (Clark and Beck, 2010: 31).

CBT has a strong commitment to scientific empiricism (Clark and Beck, 2010), i.e. seeking scientific support for CBT theory and testing the effectiveness of its clinical interventions. Scientific empiricism is not only a method but also a mindset – the willingness to abandon key CBT tenets if not supported by research evidence. Therapists are encouraged to adopt the stance of a scientist practitioner by drawing on research evidence to inform their clinical practice as well as evaluating the effectiveness of their own practice; clients are also encouraged to take an empirical stance by subjecting their problematic thoughts and beliefs to examination and reality testing in order to construct more helpful and accurate viewpoints. Therapists from other orientations argue that knowledge of human behaviour and change comes from a variety of sources (e.g. philosophy, literature, spiritual traditions), not just science; a scientific approach cannot answer all questions of importance about the human condition. In our experience, not every cognitive behaviour therapist would call him- or herself a 'strict empiricist' in the sense of being led in their clinical work only by research data (we include ourselves in this group).

Since the first edition of this book in 2004, the provision of CBT in the UK has rapidly accelerated with the government-funded initiative of improving access to psychological therapies (IAPT) in the NHS. In the IAPT programme, there are two ways of delivering CBT: high intensity that is standard CBT – the focus of this book – and reserved for clients with more severe problems; and low intensity interventions that are aimed at clients with mild to moderate psychological problems. These interventions include therapist-supported self-management such as clients using self-help workbooks and computerized CBT. Sessions are usually briefer and fewer and can be conducted face to face, by telephone, email, Skype and in groups. We work with some of our clients (we are both in private practice) in this low intensity way if they state a preference for mainly self-management of their problems. The National Institute for Health and Care Excellence (NICE), an independent body that provides guidance on which treatments to use in the NHS, recommends CBT as the first line treatment for a wide range of psychological disorders.

In this book we elaborate on 100 key points and techniques of CBT. Each elaboration is of varying length. The 100 points and techniques cover CBT theory and practice, and examine misconceptions about this approach. This book is aimed at CBT trainees and qualified practitioners, and other counsellors interested in this approach who need to be familiar with it as part of a general introduction to the current major psychotherapies. We hope that this will cover a wide readership.

Michael Neenan and Windy Dryden

Part 1

CBT THEORY

IT IS NOT EVENTS *PER SE* THAT DETERMINE OUR FEELINGS BUT THE MEANINGS THAT WE ATTACH TO THESE EVENTS

'At the very heart of the C[B]T model is the view that the human mind is not a passive receptacle of environmental and biological influences and sensations, but rather that individuals are actively involved in constructing their reality' (Clark, 1995: 156). In order to understand a person's emotional response to particular life events, it is important to discover the meaning he attaches to these events: his subjective construction of reality. For example, a person whose partner has left him believes he cannot be happy or cope on his own and becomes depressed; another person whose partner has departed feels relieved as he believes he has been freed from a 'stifling relationship'; a third person feels guilty as he views his bad behaviour as the reason for his partner's departure – the same event for each person, but not the same emotional reaction to it as each reaction is mediated by the person's view of the event; so in order to change the way we feel about events we need to change the way we think about them.

This conceptual cornerstone of cognitive behaviour therapy (CBT) derives from ancient Stoic philosophers such as Epictetus and Marcus Aurelius and their views on mental control, i.e. our thoughts and beliefs are within our control whereas many things that happen to us in life are outside of our control; therefore, we can choose how we respond to events – events themselves do not cause or dictate our emotional reactions, e.g. losing your job in a recession is outside of your control but losing your self-respect as well is a judgement you have made about being jobless (for a fascinating discussion on the links between Stoic philosophy and CBT, see Robertson, 2010).

Modern CBT does not argue that a person's emotional problems are simply created in her head but that the impact of adverse events (e.g. being burgled) can be greatly exacerbated by the person's unhelpful thoughts and beliefs that interfere with her ability to cope constructively with such events (e.g. 'I can never ever feel safe again in my own home no matter how many locks I put on the doors and windows'). CBT helps clients to develop alternative and adaptive viewpoints in order to tackle their problems (e.g. 'If I keep things in perspective, I know that the increased security measures will help to keep me safe in my home and my mind, but I realize and accept, without liking it, that there can be no guarantee I won't be burgled again'). Developing alternative viewpoints underscores the CBT principle that there is always more than one way of seeing things, no matter how unpleasant these things are. Even in the unspeakable horrors of Auschwitz, Viktor Frankl, a famous psychiatrist, observed that 'everything can be taken from a man but one thing: the last of the human freedoms – to choose one's attitude in any given set of circumstances, to choose one's own way' (1985: 86).

INFORMATION PROCESSING BECOMES DISTORTED WHEN WE EXPERIENCE EMOTIONAL DISTRESS

Cognitive theory is based on an information-processing model 'which posits that during psychological distress a person's thinking becomes more rigid and distorted, judgements become overgeneralized and absolute, and the person's basic beliefs about the self and the world become fixed' (Weishaar, 1996: 188). In an undisturbed frame of mind, a person is likely to check her impressions and appraisals of events in order to obtain clear and accurate information. When emotionally upset, the person will usually distort incoming information by introducing a consistently negative bias into her thinking so that it becomes rigid and overgeneralized, e.g. she is upset when not invited to a friend's party because she interprets the lack of an invitation as meaning that she is an unlikeable person. Instead of ascertaining the reasons for not being invited, or keeping an open mind about it, the person dwells on her supposed unlikeability, lowering her mood in the process.

Distorted thinking underlies all psychological disorders (Ledley *et al.*, 2010). These distortions usually stem from deeper dysfunctional beliefs that are activated during emotional distress, e.g. a person experiencing depression after the break-up of his relationship insists 'I'll always be alone' (fortune-telling) because he believes he is unattractive (core belief). Common information-processing errors or biases found in emotional distress include:

5

- All or nothing thinking: situations and individuals are viewed in either/or terms, e.g. 'You're either trustworthy or not. It's as simple as that'.
- Jumping to conclusions: judgements are rushed rather than considered, e.g. a client says after the first session: 'Therapy isn't helping me'.
- Mind-reading: discerning the thoughts of others without any accompanying evidence to support such claims, e.g. 'My boss didn't smile at me this morning, so that means she is unhappy with my work'.
- Labelling: attaching global negative labels to oneself, others or the world, e.g. 'I didn't understand what he said unlike others in the group, so this must mean that I'm stupid'.
- Emotional reasoning: assuming that feelings are facts, e.g. 'I feel incompetent, so it must be true' ('incompetent' is a belief, not a feeling – see Point 48).

Teaching clients how to identify and correct these errors or biases in their thinking facilitates the return of information processing that is more evidence-based, flexible and relative (non-absolute). In the example in the opening paragraph, the person discovers that her friend had invited her but 'my mother forgot to pass on the message. If I hadn't got so upset, then I wouldn't have jumped to conclusions'. If she had not been invited and it was expected that she would be, then she needs to contact her friend to find out why she has been excluded from the invitation list. Even if her friend deliberately excluded her, this does not mean the client is an unlikeable person, but a person not immune from her friendships ending and having to learn to adapt to this unwelcome reality.

3

AN EMOTIONAL DISORDER IS USUALLY UNDERSTOOD BY EXAMINING THREE LEVELS OF THINKING

These three levels of thinking are: negative automatic thoughts (NATs), underlying assumptions/rules, and core beliefs.

- NATs are situation-specific and involuntarily 'pop into' a person's mind when he is experiencing emotional distress such as depression or anxiety. They appear plausible to the person and are difficult to turn off. NATs often lie outside of immediate awareness but can be quickly brought to the client's attention by asking standard CBT questions like: 'What was going through your mind at that moment when you got to the meeting late?' (Client's reply: 'I'm always late. I'm undisciplined, sloppy. My colleagues will look down on me.') NATs can be triggered by external events and/or internal events (e.g. pounding heart: 'I'm having a heart attack. Oh God! I'm going to die'). NATs can also occur as images, e.g. a person sees himself 'dying of embarrassment' if he makes a faux pas as best man at his friend's wedding. Clients are usually more aware of how they feel than of the thoughts that prompted the feeling (Beck, 2011).
- Underlying assumptions (e.g. 'If I impress others, then I should get ahead in life') and rules (e.g. 'I should not let people down') guide behaviour, set standards and provide rules to follow. These assumptions and rules are often unarticulated and can be difficult for clients to detect. Underlying assumptions are usually identified by their 'if

7

... then' or 'unless ... then' construction, and rules are usually expressed in 'must' and 'should' statements. These assumptions and rules are the means by which individuals hope to avoid coming 'face to face' with their negative core beliefs (e.g. 'I'm incompetent'). The 'truth' of these core beliefs is not questioned and, therefore, assumptions and rules serve to maintain and reinforce them. Trouble looms for the person when behaviour is not what it should be, standards are not met or rules are violated; 'trouble' is the activation of the negative core belief from its dormant state. Beck *et al.* (1985) suggest that maladaptive assumptions often focus on three major issues: acceptance (e.g. 'I'm nothing unless I'm loved'), competence (e.g. 'I am what I accomplish') and control (e.g. 'I can't ask for help'). Assumptions and rules are cross-situational and are also known as intermediate beliefs because they lie between NATs and core beliefs (Beck, 2011).

- Core beliefs (also known as schemas; see below) are the third level of thought and the deepest. Negative core beliefs are overgeneralized and unconditional (e.g. 'I'm hopeless'). They are usually formed through early learning experiences and lie dormant until activated by relevant life events (e.g. the client sees himself as incompetent for not living up to his standards of being efficient, punctual and disciplined). Once activated, negative core beliefs process information in a biased way that confirms them and disconfirms contradictory information (e.g. 'So what if I'm mostly on time for meetings?'). Core beliefs can be about the self (e.g. 'I'm unloveable'), others (e.g. 'I can't trust anyone'), and/or the world (e.g. 'Everything is against me'). Once the distress has passed, negative core beliefs become deactivated or return to their latent state and a more positive outlook is re-established (clients with personality disorders may have their negative core beliefs activated most of the time; see Davidson, 2008).

How do these three levels interact? A person feels depressed when he fails to get 'A' grades in his exams. His dormant core belief, 'I'm a failure', is activated by his inability to live up to his rigid rule of living that he must be the best at everything he does and his mind is flooded with NATs: 'I can't show my face at college. Run away and hide. The whole college is laughing at me.' Working at the NATs level provides symptom relief while tackling maladaptive assumptions/rules and negative core beliefs reduce a client's vulnerability in experiencing future episodes of emotional disturbance. The usual treatment strategy in CBT is early intervention at the NATs level and then moving on to underlying assumptions/rules and core beliefs.

It is important to point out that not every client problem will have this three-level examination. Short-term CBT may focus primarily on modifying NATs (and also helping indirectly to reactivate the client's existing positive core beliefs that are temporarily inactive); unhelpful assumptions and rules are pinpointed when problems are recurrent while core beliefs are usually the main target when treating problems requiring longer-term therapy. Dobson and Dobson (2009) suggest that it is quite likely that negative core beliefs change gradually without directly modifying them if clients continue to think and act differently over the longer term.

We would like to end this point on a technical note about schemas and core beliefs. Cognitive schemas 'are organized structures of stored information that contain individual's perceptions of self and others, goals, expectations and memories' (Beck and Dozois, 2011). Core beliefs (e.g. 'I'm no good' and 'People cannot be trusted') represent the content of the schemas. As these examples of negative core beliefs suggest, CBT focuses on maladaptive cognitive schemas that process incoming information in negatively biased and rigid ways. For some CBT writers these terms, schemas and core beliefs, can be used interchangeably because 'although schemas are the core of the cognitive framework, they can be verbalized in the form of beliefs' (Dobson, 2012: 82). We also use these terms interchangeably throughout this book.

THOUGHTS, FEELINGS, BEHAVIOUR, PHYSIOLOGY AND ENVIRONMENT ARE INTERCONNECTED

In the cognitive model, uncovering the meaning (thoughts and beliefs) that clients' attach to events is critical for understanding their emotional and behavioural reactions to these events. However, cognition in CBT is not viewed in isolation from other response systems within the person but recognizes its interaction with her behaviour, physiology and emotions; and these systems interact with the wider context of her environment such as living in a high crime neighbourhood and having noisy neighbours. Each one of these elements is capable of influencing the others in an interactive cycle. Greenberger and Padesky (1995) suggest that understanding how these five aspects of a person's life experience are interconnected can help the client to understand her problems better. For example, a client who loses her job (environment) sees herself as worthless (belief), feels depressed (emotion), withdraws from social activity (behaviour) and complains of constant tiredness (physiology). A change in one of these elements, such as a return to being sociable, produces positive change in the other four: the client looks for another job (environment), sees herself again as a person of worth (belief), her depressed mood lifts (emotion) and she starts to feel re-energized (physiology).

Sometimes others in the client's environment (e.g. her partner) may be encouraged to attend therapy if her problems are to be addressed adequately. Cultural messages may have an adverse impact on the client's difficulties such as 'size zero' thinking in the fashion industry (e.g. 'Being thin is everything') and will need to be addressed as they are bound up with the client's negative self-view.

In CBT, the usual 'way in' to help a client's understanding of this interactive process is by identifying his situation-specific NATs, e.g. 'Do you know what you were thinking [thoughts] in that situation [environment] that made you feel so jittery [physiology] and anxious [emotion] that you rushed [behaviour] out of the room?' Teaching this interactive process does not undermine a core proposition in CBT: that cognitive change is central to the human change process (Clark and Steer, 1996).

EMOTIONAL REACTIONS TO EVENTS ARE VIEWED ALONG A CONTINUUM

CBT suggests that there is continuity between 'normal' emotional reactions to life events and excessive or extreme emotional reactions found in psychopathology (disturbances in thoughts, feelings and behaviours). As Weishaar and Beck explain:

> The cognitive content of syndromes (e.g. anxiety disorders, depression) have the same theme (e.g. danger or loss, respectively) as found in 'normal' experience, but cognitive distortions are extreme and, consequently, so are affect [emotion] and behaviour.
> (1986: 65)

For example, a person looking over his life might experience sadness at the wasted opportunities but knows that new opportunities lie ahead; however, his sadness may intensify and become a prolonged depression if he sees such wasted opportunities as the whole story of his life. With physiological reactions (e.g. heart pounding, sweating, trembling), they would be the same for a person who believed he was about to be attacked (physical threat) as for a person who feared making mistakes in front of others (psychosocial threat).

Normal and exaggerated emotional reactions to events are characterized, respectively, by what Beck *et al.* (1979) call 'mature' (flexible) and 'primitive' (absolute) thinking. For example, a mature response to being disliked might be that 'you can't please everyone' whereas a primitive response might conclude that 'I'm thoroughly unlikeable'. Explaining to clients this continuum of emotional reactions to life events helps to remove some of the stigma from psychological distress and thereby normalizes it. This normalizing process helps clients to see that they are not 'weirdos' or 'uniquely abnormal' for experiencing episodes of extreme emotional distress.

EMOTIONAL DISORDERS HAVE A SPECIFIC COGNITIVE CONTENT

Also known as the content-specificity hypothesis (Beck, 1976), this hypothesis proposes that emotional disorders have a specific cognitive content or theme running through them. For example, devaluation or loss in depression, danger or threat in anxiety, situationally specific danger in phobia, transgression in anger, and expansion in happiness. These themes are tied to Beck's concept of the 'personal domain', i.e. anything that the person considers important in her life. The nature of 'a person's emotional response – or emotional disturbance – depends on whether he perceives events as adding to, subtracting from, endangering, or impinging upon his domain' (Beck, 1976: 56). Some examples will help to explain this relationship:

- A person who prides herself on being a successful businesswoman becomes depressed when her company goes bust because she believes, 'My work is my life. Without my company, I'm nothing' (subtraction).
- A person becomes anxious that his sexual prowess will be ridiculed when he experiences erectile dysfunction (endangerment).
- A person is delighted that she has been promoted as this is now another significant step in her career path (expansion).
- A person who enjoys peace and quiet in his life becomes very angry when his new next-door neighbour plays her music very loud (impingement).

A person may experience different emotions to the same event on separate occasions depending on the event's relevance to his personal domain, e.g. anxious on Monday when the train is late as he will then be late for a meeting that might undermine his personal standard of punctuality (endangerment), while on Tuesday he is angry when the train is late as it means more people will board the train at his station thereby restricting his personal space on the train (impingement). The content-specificity hypothesis was validated by empirical research in the 1980s (Weishaar, 1996).

COGNITIVE VULNERABILITY TO EMOTIONAL DISTURBANCE

Vulnerability can be defined as an 'endogenous [internal], stable characteristic that remains latent until activated by a precipitating event' (Clark and Beck, 2010: 102). An event that may trigger vulnerability in one person (e.g. receiving a poor performance appraisal) is viewed with equanimity by another. Beck (1987) proposed two broad personality types who would be at risk for depression or anxiety: sociotropy and autonomy.

> The sociotropic personality orientation places a high value on having close interpersonal relations, with a strong emphasis on being loved and valued by others. On the other hand, the autonomous personality orientation reflects a high investment in personal independence, achievement, and freedom of choice.
>
> (Clark and Steer, 1996: 81)

A typical sociotropic belief is 'I must be loved in order to be happy', while a typical autonomous belief is 'I must be a success in order to be worthwhile' (Beck, 1987). Anxiety can occur if, for example, there is a perceived threat to a close relationship or the danger of a career setback; if this perceived danger or threat is realized, then depression is likely to ensue. The match between a person's specific vulnerability (e.g. sees herself as worthless unless she is loved) and a significant life event that reflects this belief (e.g. her partner leaves her) is likened by Beck (1987) to a key fitting into a lock to open the door to depression; technically speaking, 'Cognitive theory is essentially a diathesis-stress model' (Beck and Dozois, 2011) where the diathesis is the cognitive vulnerability (maladaptive beliefs) and the stress is current adverse life events (precipitating factors) that activate these beliefs. Scott (2009) points out that there are varying degrees of vulnerability, so a number of adverse life events may need to occur rather than just one before depression descends, e.g. for an autonomous person, failing to achieve important life goals, and becoming ill and dependent.

8

OUR THOUGHTS AND BELIEFS ARE BOTH KNOWABLE AND ACCESSIBLE

Between an external stimulus (e.g. being criticized) and an emotional response to it (e.g. anger) lie a person's thoughts about this event. Eliciting these thoughts helps the person to understand why she reacted in the way that she did to the event. Beck calls this 'tapping the internal communications' and states that clients can be trained 'to focus on their introspections [examining one's thoughts] in various situations. The person can then observe that a thought links the external stimulus with the emotional response' (1976: 27). Asking a client such questions as 'What was going through your mind at that moment?' or 'What were you thinking about in that situation?' can help to turn her attention inwards rather than remain focused on the external event that she might assume 'caused' her emotional reaction. In the above example, the person is able to uncover her thoughts which contributed to her anger: 'How dare he criticize me! I've done nothing wrong to deserve this. He's a bastard!' Helping a client to detect, examine and change his disturbance-producing thoughts means that this process can be accomplished 'within the scope of his own awareness' (Beck, 1976: 3) rather than such thoughts remaining inaccessible to him.

A client might experience an emotional response without an obvious external stimulus to trigger it; in this case, the client needs to search for an internal stimulus such as an image (e.g. seeing herself stammering in front of an audience) or a memory (e.g. being shouted at by a schoolteacher) in order to understand why her feeling seemed to 'come out of the blue'.

In Point 3, we described three levels of cognition (negative automatic thoughts [NATs], assumptions/rules, and core beliefs) in understanding emotional disorders. These levels usually correspond with the degree of difficulty in gaining access to them. Surface thoughts (NATs) are usually on the fringe of awareness, though they can be quickly brought 'centre stage' in the client's mind by asking the questions already mentioned above. Underlying assumptions/rules and core beliefs often remain unarticulated and, therefore, can be more difficult to gain access to. Linking NATs to underlying (intermediate and core) beliefs is achieved by asking the client to probe for the logical implications of each NAT (e.g. 'If it's true that you cry easily, what does that mean to you?') until important rules (e.g. 'I should always be strong') and core beliefs (e.g. 'I'm weak') are uncovered. Peeling away layers of personal meaning makes explicit what was previously implicit.

ACQUISITION OF EMOTIONAL DISTURBANCE

CBT does not claim that dysfunctional thinking alone causes emotional distress; rather it forms an integral part of this distress. Psychological disturbance is multiply determined by, among other things, genetic, environmental, familial, cultural, personality and developmental factors. The interplay between these factors helps to form a person's idiosyncratic core beliefs, assumptions and rules about themselves, others and the world. These predisposing factors interact with relevant current events or stressors (precipitating factors) to trigger emotional disturbance. For example, a person who comes from a very competitive academic family is told by his parents that he will never be as clever as his brothers; so he spends his time trying to prove them wrong. When he fails to get into Oxford University, unlike his two brothers, and has to settle for a 'second-class' university, his core beliefs, 'I'm not clever enough. My parents are right: I'm the idiot in the family', are activated leading to the development of depression accompanied by social withdrawal, heavy drinking and poor academic performance. Therefore, to speak of cognitions causing emotional disorders without taking any other factors into consideration (e.g. childhood neglect, oversensitive nature, social isolation) is misleading:

> We consider that the primary pathology or dysfunction during a depression or an anxiety disorder is in the cognitive apparatus. However, that is quite different from the notion that cognition *causes* these syndromes – a notion that is just as illogical as an assertion that hallucinations cause schizophrenia.
>
> (Beck *et al.*, 1985: 85; emphasis in original)

The 'cognitive apparatus' would be the activation of negative core beliefs (e.g. 'I'm repulsive') which filter information about the person's experiences (e.g. 'No one ever wants to go out with me') in a biased and distorted way, serving to reinforce and perpetuate these core beliefs and intensify the emotional distress associated with them.

MAINTENANCE OF EMOTIONAL DISTURBANCE

CBT 'considers *current* cognitive functioning crucial to the maintenance and persistence of psychological disturbance' (Clark, 1995: 158; emphasis in original). By staying mainly in the present, the therapist helps the client to modify her current maladaptive thoughts (e.g. 'I can't be happy without him'), assumptions (e.g. 'If he's abandoned me, then no one else will ever want me') and core beliefs (e.g. 'I'm unloveable') in order to ameliorate her emotional disturbance. Historical factors (e.g. parental neglect, bullied at school, severe acne during adolescence) that contributed to the person's current problems (e.g. low self-esteem) cannot be modified; current beliefs and behaviours that maintain these problems can be.

A historical perspective is usually included in therapy as it helps the therapist to understand how the client's present difficulties developed and the nature of her specific vulnerabilities to emotional distress. Also, the client may blame past events for her current problems (e.g. 'My parents always told me that I would be left on the shelf. It's their fault I am the way that I am'). However, the therapist would redirect the client's attention to the present where she continues to subscribe to these destructive parental messages, and encourage her to focus on what steps she can take to develop helpful and compassionate self-messages.

Behaviour plays a very important role in maintaining emotional distress as individuals act in ways that support their dysfunctional beliefs – you act as you think. For example, a client with depression sees himself as weak and unable to cope on his own; he acts in a 'helpless' way by trailing around after his wife expecting to be told what to do by her. Behaviour change would involve the client acting against his dysfunctional beliefs by gradually making more of his own decisions about how to spend his time productively. By changing his behaviour, the client eventually realizes that his negative self-image was part of the depression, not the 'truth' about himself. In summary, cognitive and behaviour change are equally important (hence CBT).

11

THE CLIENT AS PERSONAL SCIENTIST

This refers to helping clients to 'learn how to become scientific investigators of their own thinking – to treat thoughts as hypotheses rather than as facts and to put these thoughts to the test' (Beck and Dozois, 2011). For example, a depressed client, who predicts that none of his friends will return his phone calls because they no longer care about him, makes six phone calls, three of which are returned, and grudgingly concedes that there could be benign reasons why the other three did not contact him (even if these three are no longer interested in him, it only proves that his prediction was partly true).

The image of therapy that the cognitive behavioural therapist wants to convey to her client is that of two scientists working together to define the latter's problem, to formulate and test hypotheses about it and find problem-solving options (Blackburn and Davidson, 1995). Beck *et al.* (1979) call this working together as two scientists or co-investigators 'collaborative empiricism'. Working as co-investigators into problem-solving guards against the possibility of the relationship becoming one of guru and disciple – this partnership in problem-solving provides the success in therapy, not the therapist; also this working together disabuses clients of the notion that the therapist's job is to 'fix me' while they remain passive in the 'fixing' process.

Poor science can occur in this collaborative enterprise if the therapist wants only to confirm her hypotheses about the client's problems (e.g. 'It's definitely an approval issue') and the client continually discounts the data that contradict his negative beliefs (e.g. 'Successes don't count, failure does;

therefore, I'm a failure'). Developing and maintaining open-mindedness means that both therapist and client speak from the collected data rather than from personal opinion or prejudice.

Part 2

MISCONCEPTIONS ABOUT CBT

ONLY ARTICULATE AND INTELLIGENT CLIENTS CAN REALLY BENEFIT FROM CBT

CBT clients are, ideally, expected to provide detailed information about their problems; fill out inventories to obtain baseline measures regarding the severity of their presenting problems; detect their dysfunctional thinking and its relationship to their emotional distress; fill in forms to identify and distinguish between situations, thoughts and feelings; use reason and reality testing to challenge dysfunctional thinking; negotiate, carry out and review homework assignments; and provide feedback on their learning and experiences of therapy. At first blush, this seems like a highly intellectual endeavour that only the most intelligent and articulate clients will benefit from.

However, as Beck *et al.* (1979) observe, high intelligence is not required from either the client or therapist (IQ tests are not applied to either!). The important point is that the therapist adapts CBT to the intellectual and verbal abilities of each client. For example, getting rid of jargon (some therapists might think it makes them sound more authoritative), having shorter sessions, keeping paperwork to a minimum, providing simple explanations of CBT theory and practice, and action assignments taking precedence over cognitive tasks if the client finds introspection too difficult or unhelpful.

CBT has been shown to be effective with clients from different social and educational backgrounds (Persons *et al.*, 1988) and has been adapted for working with, among others, older people (Laidlaw *et al.*, 2003), learning disabilities (Kroese *et al.*, 1997), children and young people (Stallard, 2002), and adult male offenders (Altrows, 2002).

CBT DOES NOT FOCUS ON FEELINGS

The word 'cognitive' may give the impression that cognitive behaviour therapists focus only on thoughts and exclude feelings. This is untrue as emotions are the starting point for therapeutic intervention – after all, clients usually come to therapy complaining of how they are feeling, not about what they are thinking. Thoughts and feelings are continually linked in therapy by the therapist teaching the cognitive model and the client filling in the daily thought record (DTR) forms (see Appendix 2). As Blackburn and Davidson emphasize:

> Cognitive therapy cannot progress without taking emotions into consideration *at all times*. If the patient cannot have access to his painful emotions, he and the therapist will not be able to elicit the negative thoughts which need attending to. Put simply, cognitive therapy *cannot* take place without first eliciting relevant emotional reactions.
>
> (1995: 203; emphases in original)

The first cognitive therapy treatment manual, *Cognitive Therapy of Depression* (Beck *et al.*, 1979), contained a chapter called 'The role of emotions in cognitive therapy' and stressed that the therapist 'needs to be able to empathize with the patient's painful emotional experiences' (1979: 35). Trying to keep emotions out of therapy might suggest that the real focus in CBT is on teaching the client how to develop a more logical mind to aid problem-solving; and if this was true then Beck's 1976 book, *Cognitive Therapy and the Emotional Disorders*, had been wrongly titled and should have been called 'Cognitive Therapy and the Thinking Disorders'.

Emotion needs to be activated in the sessions in order to gain access to a client's 'hot' (emotionally charged) cognitions, which will then enable cognitive restructuring (thought and belief change) to begin. For example, a client relives a situation where she continues to feel intense guilt over a 'one night stand' with a friend of her husband's and considers herself 'thoroughly bad' for what she has done; helping the client to distinguish between the act and herself (the act does not define the whole person or her life) reduced the intensity of her guilt. Therefore, 'the thoughts and beliefs important in cognitive therapy are emotional – they deal with our emotions and not our intellect' (Clark and Beck, 2012: 57).

The therapist 'should be skilled at eliciting affect [emotion] if the client does not express it spontaneously' (Dattilio and Padesky, 1990: 2). Emotional change (e.g. 'How would you like to feel instead of angry all the time?') is fundamental to the practice of CBT: 'The success of CT is in part judged by reductions in negative emotional responses like sadness and fear, as well as concomitant increases in positive emotions' (Clark, 1995: 160).

CBT IS BASICALLY POSITIVE THINKING

If your partner leaves you, do not worry because you will find another one soon. If you are criticized by your manager, just put it down to her bad mood. Some therapists might believe that positive thinking will automatically lead to positive feelings. Leahy (2003) warns against the therapist becoming a cheerleader for positive thinking. How does the therapist know the client will find another partner soon or the manager did not mean her criticism? Clients are likely to become irritated with the therapist's sunny reassurance. Therefore, CBT 'is not the replacement of negative thoughts with positive ones; rather, it aims to help individuals shift their cognitive appraisals from ones that are unhealthy and maladaptive to ones that are evidence-based and adaptive' (Beck and Dozois, 2011). These new appraisals are developed through exploring clients' idiosyncratic meanings they attach to events, examining alternative viewpoints with which to view these events, and executing experiments to test the validity of their thoughts and beliefs.

For example, a client who claims that his professional credibility has been 'destroyed' after experiencing a panic attack in front of a large audience would not be reassured by the therapist that 'everyone still thinks well of you and your reputation is still intact'. Instead, she would encourage the client to look at the evidence for and against his belief that his credibility has been destroyed: e.g. respectively, 'Some people told me to "chuck it in" to avoid future embarrassment' versus 'The feedback I get is generally just as good as it was before the panic attack'. Based on the evidence, his credibility has been diminished in some people's eyes, though certainly not everyone's, and he decides to continue with his public speaking engagements.

Positive thinking (e.g. 'I can achieve anything I want') should not be confused with a positive outlook (e.g. 'Whatever bad things happen in my life, I can usually find a way forward so I'm not particularly worried about this latest setback'): the former outlook relies on an unjustifiable optimism which banishes any disagreeable facts that may need to be faced, whereas the latter one is based on assessing accurately the behavioural evidence to date.

15

CBT SEEMS TOO SIMPLE

This misconception often arises because of the confusion between the meanings of 'simple' and 'simplistic': straightforward versus over-simple. CBT is not simplistic; it attempts to follow the law of parsimony or Ockham's razor: 'If you can explain something adequately without introducing further complexity, then the simple explanation is the best explanation' (Warburton, 2007: 107). The therapist attempts to follow Ockham's razor by looking for simple explanations and solutions rather than complex ones (though the therapist can walk a fine line at times in trying to distinguish between simple and simplistic explanations of clients' problems).

For example, a client complains of feeling angry when her boss gives her extra work (e.g. 'It's not bloody fair! Because I finish my work first, I get punished for being efficient'). Understanding and moderating the client's anger will not usually be advanced by her attempting to pinpoint her boss's putative motives, developing a psychological profile of him and/or discussing repeatedly the corporate culture. Helping the client to see that she is not exempt from experiencing unfairness in the workplace (or anywhere else) and addressing her concerns to her boss may prove to be straightforward solutions to her anger problem. If further complexity is added to the case conceptualization, this is based on evidence that such an approach is needed, not on the therapist's belief that complexity and depth in problem investigation means you are a 'real' therapist rather than a 'tinkerer' with surface issues.

With regard to the surface, Beck was keen on stressing that 'there's more to the surface than meets the eye'. What he meant by this was that the client's automatic thoughts (the raw material as Beck called them [1976], e.g. 'There's no excuse for failure') could be taken at face value to understand her emotional reaction (e.g. anxiety) to events (e.g. falling behind on a work project) and therapy could be conducted successfully at this surface level by examining and correcting these distortions in her thinking in order to improve her mood.

When further complexity is necessary, explanations still follow the law of parsimony in 'specifying the simplest *sufficient* explanation for a stated purpose' (Naugle and Follette, 1998: 67; emphasis in original). For example, long-standing problems can cluster around the belief 'I'm a phoney and will eventually be found out for what I really am' which the client (introduced in the second paragraph) finds sufficient and satisfactory in explaining why she drives herself relentlessly to finish her work first to prove to her boss how efficient she is and thereby, in her mind, keeps pushing back the day of 'exposure' as a fraud.

16

CBT IS LITTLE MORE THAN SYMPTOM RELIEF

CBT can be relatively brief: between 6–20 sessions (Westbrook *et al.*, 2011). This appears to some therapists from other orientations that CBT offers only symptom relief for clients' problems instead of embarking on the required lengthy investigations of the root causes of these problems which are usually traced to childhood experiences (non-cognitive behavioural therapists often see their views of root causes as facts derived from the theories they espouse rather than as hypotheses in need of scientific scrutiny). As a result of this 'superficial' approach, only a sticking plaster has been put on these problems and, consequently, they will inevitably recur. In CBT, current thoughts and beliefs (maintaining factors) can be seen as cognitive 'root causes' (Clark and Beck, 2012). As we discussed in Point 3, a client's problems can be understood by examining three cognitive levels: surface or situation-specific negative automatic thoughts (NATs), cross-situational rules and assumptions (intermediate beliefs) and unconditional core beliefs. The deeper the cognitive level, the more difficult it can be to gain access to and change.

However, it does not automatically follow that every client problem has to be viewed through these three levels or that the client will want to stay in therapy for deeper exploration of her problems once she starts feeling better. She may disagree that there are any underlying issues to resolve (e.g. 'I got what I came for'), and what was a collaborative relationship can turn into a coercive one if the therapist insists on the client staying in therapy for 'deeper work', i.e. non-symptom focused.

The degree of complexity introduced into therapy is suggested by the clinical circumstances of each case, not by a predetermined view that every problem requires a depth-centred approach. For example, a client with panic disorder can use a well-established and empirically based treatment programme (e.g. Salkovskis and Clark, 1991) that is likely to help him become panic-free at the end of treatment and with his therapeutic gains being maintained at follow-up (Clark, 1996) without necessarily having to explore underlying (intermediate and core) belief levels as part of the programme.

On the other hand, in working with clients with personality disorders (i.e. rigid personality traits: e.g. avoidant, dependent, histrionic; chronic maladaptive behaviour, and poor interpersonal functioning), Young *et al.* (2003) proposed a schema-focused approach with a 'primary emphasis on the deepest level of cognition, the early [childhood] maladaptive schema [core belief, e.g. "I am bad"]'. To promote client change at this level, therapy needs to be long-term with the length of treatment likely to take 12 months or more (Davidson, 2008).

Within CBT there is disagreement about the use of and need for schema-focused approaches for clients with uncomplicated clinical problems which can be complicated by such approaches (James, 2001). For example, instead of being offered an anxiety management package to cope with major changes at work, a client suffering from acute anxiety about these changes is steered by an over-enthusiastic therapist into schema work which uncovers a core belief ('I'm no good') which the client neither knew he had nor sees the relevance of working on. This eagerness for schema-focused approaches 'is particularly worrying owing to the fact that, despite being far more intrusive, there is little evidence that they are more effective than non-schema interventions' (James, 2001: 404). Whether symptom reduction or elimination is sufficient help for the client or as a prelude to working at deeper cognitive levels, the level of clinical intrusion should match the requirements of the presenting problem, not the interests of the therapist.

CBT IS NOT INTERESTED IN THE CLIENT'S PAST OR CHILDHOOD EXPERIENCES

CBT is an ahistorical (here and now) problem-solving approach: the client's distressing feelings are ameliorated by him identifying and changing his current maladaptive thinking and behaviour that serves to maintain these feelings rather than by him exploring and blaming unchangeable past events for these feelings (if the client has been in a therapy which focuses on the past, he may experience considerable difficulty in reorientating himself to the present). However, clinical attention

> Shifts to the past in two circumstances. One, when patients express a strong preference to do so, and a failure to do so could endanger the therapeutic alliance. Two, when patients get "stuck" in their dysfunctional thinking, and an understanding of the childhood roots of their beliefs can potentially help them modify their rigid ideas.
>
> (Beck, 2011: 8)

Clinical attention may shift to the past but it does not usually dwell there. With the client's 'strong preference' for exploration of the past, the therapist can help him to make connections with past adverse events (e.g. 'Being betrayed by my best friend') to his current thinking and behaviour about these events (e.g. 'Since that time, I've never really been able to trust another friend and that's why I keep my distance'). When there is little, if any, therapeutic movement (e.g. the client expresses no sense of relief or freedom about leaving an abusive relationship) this may be due to the client being fixated on 'Why?' questions (e.g. 'Why did I get involved with him? Why did I put up with it for so long? How can I be happy if I don't understand why I behaved that way?'). Looking back in order to answer these questions may not produce the satisfying answers the client is looking for or, if satisfying answers are found, break the logjam in therapy: old questions may be answered, but new beliefs and behaviours are needed to avoid the possibility of the past repeating itself in the next relationship or impairing her new-found independence.

Sometimes the therapist will direct the client's attention to the past in order to help her see that what she considers to be 'true' about herself (e.g. 'I'm not good enough. My parents favoured my older sisters over me') was formed in response to being brought up in a family environment where she had to compete with her two older sisters for parental praise and affection. The parents believed that rewards were to be given to whichever daughter showed the most hard work and determination in, for example, completing their school homework or helping around the house. The client frequently lost out in this fierce competition. The legacy of that environment remains with her today in her endless striving to prove herself 'good enough' but, when falling short, confirms in her mind 'the truth about myself'.

The client was shown the various ways she has maintained and strengthened this belief over the years thereby, in her mind, continually confirming its truth. Now, in therapy, she is developing a new belief which is self-nurturing, balanced and compassionate (e.g. 'I'm learning that I'm good enough based on my own reasonable terms for conducting my own life in my own way') which helps to mitigate her painful childhood memories (see Point 90). While the learning history behind a client's dysfunctional beliefs may need to be explored, the 'crucial thing is for him or her to give up these currently held ideas so that tomorrow's existence can [begin to] be better than yesterday's' (Grieger and Boyd, 1980: 76–77).

18

CBT DOES NOT MAKE USE OF THE RELATIONSHIP AS A MEANS OF CLIENT CHANGE

The standard view of the therapeutic relationship in CBT is that it is necessary to help promote client change but not sufficient to produce optimum change – this is achieved through the execution of cognitive and behavioural techniques (Beck *et al.*, 1979). These techniques are applied to the client's problems that occur outside of therapy, and only applied to the relationship itself when difficulties within it prevent the successful implementation of these techniques (these difficulties were called by Beck *et al.* [1979] 'technical problems'). Later developments in CBT viewed 'the relationship … as an intervention tool in itself' (Blackburn and Twaddle, 1996: 7). An example of the 'relationship as an intervention tool' is its use with clients who have personality disorders where the therapy relationship becomes 'a schema laboratory in which the client can safely evaluate maladaptive core beliefs [e.g. "No one can be trusted"]' (Padesky and Greenberger, 1995: 123; Beck *et al.*, 2004), and test out alternative and more adaptive core beliefs (e.g. 'Some people can be trusted sometimes'). Since clients with personality disorders often have difficulty in developing a therapeutic relationship, the 'laboratory' allows the therapist to observe the client's interpersonal functioning closely as well as gaining a historical account of persistent difficulties in other relationships (Davidson, 2008).

Exploring interpersonal processes can help the therapist to understand and tackle the issues of transference, countertransference and impasses in the therapeutic relationship which hinder client progress; if some cognitive behavioural therapists object to the psychodynamic terms of transference and countertransference being used in CBT, they can, for example, choose 'therapy-interfering beliefs and behaviours' as being more CBT-oriented. Transference means 'that patients react (and more important, overreact) to the therapist as they do to other significant people in their lives' (Walen *et al.*, 1992: 246). For example, the client may always defer to the expertise of the therapist, as she does to other authority figures in her life, instead of thinking things through for herself: 'My opinions don't count.' Such 'dependent thinking' will undermine the client's ability to become her own self-therapist – the ultimate goal of CBT. The therapist can facilitate her movement towards more independent thinking by continually reinforcing the message that her 'opinions do count and that's why I want to hear your views'.

Countertransference is how the therapist thinks and feels about her client; e.g. she feels a sense of dread about the approach of the client's appointment time as she will have to endure 'an hour of moaning and whining'. With the help of a competent supervisor she can learn to endure each appointment without dread (e.g. 'The clients are not here to entertain me or make my life easy'), and look for creative ways to shift the client from 'whining' about his problems to working on them. Impasses in the therapeutic relationship (e.g. disagreements over the pace of therapy) can be resolved through what Safran and Muran (2000) call 'metacommunication' – i.e. the client and therapist stepping outside of the strained relationship in order to comment upon it in a non-blaming spirit of collaborative inquiry (e.g. the therapist agrees to moderate his 'hurry up' approach to problem-solving and the client agrees to provide more specific information about her problem rather than keep talking in general terms about it). The therapist carries the main responsibility for initiating and maintaining the metacommunication process.

In summary, while there is much discussion in the research literature over the relative importance assigned to the relationship or treatment techniques, Leahy suggests 'that assuring the use of cognitive therapy techniques and improving the therapeutic alliance may provide the optimal treatment' (2008: 770).

19

CBT IS NOT INTERESTED IN THE SOCIAL AND ENVIRONMENTAL FACTORS THAT CONTRIBUTE TO CLIENTS' PROBLEMS

This misconception assumes that CBT takes the purely cognitive view that distorted thinking alone creates a person's emotional distress irrespective of his life circumstances; therefore, the client is to blame for his problems for 'thinking incorrectly'. Not so. CBT is 'directed at correcting the combination of psychological and *situational* problems which may be contributing to the patient's distress' (Blackburn and Davidson, 1995: 16; emphasis added). The therapist investigates both worlds of the client, internal and external (the daily thought record [DTR] form requires situational information as well as thoughts and feelings; see Appendix 2). For example, with a client who felt 'trapped in an unhappy marriage and I've got to get out' the therapist would want to understand what makes the marriage unhappy for the client (e.g. 'My husband is an alcoholic. I don't know him any longer and love has died') and what thoughts and feelings keep her trapped within it (e.g. 'If I leave him, he'll just drink himself to death and it'll be my fault. I'll feel so guilty').

A ludicrous view of CBT would be that the client is upset solely by her negative thinking about living with an alcoholic and that the debilitating effects of such a relationship have no effect on her psychological state. In real-life CBT, the therapist would acknowledge the client's dilemma and collaboratively conduct a realistic appraisal of her 'responsibility' for his death if she left him and her prediction came true: 'I have no power to stop him drinking whether I live with him or leave him.' By moderating her guilt feelings, the client is able, with much sadness, to leave the relationship.

In essence, cognitive behaviour therapists want to understand, in collaboration with their clients, how objectively unpleasant situations can be made worse by the clients' distorted and unrealistic appraisals which then impair their ability to cope adaptively with these difficulties.

20

CBT IS JUST THE APPLICATION OF COMMON SENSE TO CLIENTS' PROBLEMS

This means that CBT simply encourages clients to think realistically about their problems instead of blowing them up out of all proportion; once common-sense thinking prevails, then emotional relief will be achieved. Beck's (1976) book, *Cognitive Therapy and the Emotional Disorders*, contains a chapter called 'Common Sense and Beyond' in which he says that each person 'by virtue of his personal experience, emulation of others, and formal education ... learns how to use the tools of common sense: forming and testing hunches, making discriminations, and reasoning' (1976: 12–13). The therapist can encourage her clients to draw on their common sense in tackling their emotional problems.

However, common sense has its limits and fails 'to provide plausible and useful explanations for the puzzling emotional disorders' (Beck, 1976: 24). For example, a client may have had hundreds of panic attacks in which he believed that his pounding heart signalled an imminent heart attack but, on each occasion, no attack occurred. The client has a tremendous amount of evidence to disconfirm his catastrophic prediction but no such disconfirmation has taken place. Why has his common sense failed him so many times on this issue? Also, common-sense advice from his family and friends (e.g. 'If you were going to have a heart attack, you would have had one by now, so there's nothing to worry about, is there?') also fails to reassure him. To find the answer to this puzzle requires the uncommon sense of the therapist-as-detective in uncovering the factors that maintain the client's panic-stricken thinking.

Salkovskis (1991) points to the importance of safety behaviours in maintaining anxiety and panic (i.e. behaviours which prevent the feared catastrophe from occurring). In the above example, when the client's heart is pounding he may try to relax, sit down, take deep breaths, avoid exercise or strenuous activity in order to slow down his heart rate and thereby, in his mind, avert a heart attack. Unfortunately, his common-sense approach to saving himself actually strengthens or 'protects' his catastrophic predictions (e.g. 'That was a close one. Next time I might not be so lucky.') because each panic attack is viewed as a 'near miss' (Wells, 1997) rather than as evidence that his thoughts are incorrect; so the client believes he has had hundreds of 'near misses'. Once the client's internal logic related to his safety behaviours is revealed, he can drop these behaviours – stop trying to save himself! – and undertake experiments when feeling panicky (e.g. running on the spot or up and down stairs with the therapist, and then carry out these exercises on his own when alone) in order to see what actually happens to him and thereby draw new and non-dangerous conclusions about his pounding heart (e.g. 'My heart is fine').

The client may reflect that what he has learnt in therapy 'just seems like common sense really', but it did not seem like common sense before he learnt it as he was initially fearful about dropping his safety behaviours and wondered if the therapist was 'mad' in suggesting it to him.

21

CBT IS JUST TECHNIQUE-ORIENTED

A common criticism of CBT 'is that it appears too "technique-oriented" – that is, too focused on a nontheoretical, or nonceptual approach to the individual patient' (Leahy *et al.*, 2012: 437). This misconception assumes that cognitive behaviour therapists simply consult their treatment manuals for particular disorders (e.g. panic, obsessive compulsive disorder) and apply the recommended evidence-based techniques to achieve amelioration of clients' symptoms. In fact, the application of techniques comes after a case conceptualization (or formulation) of the client's presenting problems has been developed collaboratively (see Point 30). Derived from the cognitive theory of emotional disorders, a case conceptualization is a highly individualized understanding of a client's problem in terms of its development, (e.g. the client was terrified when she got lost for several hours driving to Liverpool for the first time – 'It was a truly awful experience'); what circumstances activate her high anxiety (e.g. anticipating or actually getting lost when travelling to new destinations, sometimes being unconfident about reaching safely familiar places); and how the problem is being maintained (e.g. trying to be absolutely certain that the travel directions are correct in every respect; excessive pre-travel worry). Installing Sat Nav made little impact on reducing her anxiety because it might malfunction thereby getting her lost. In the cognitive theory of anxiety, the theme is of a future threat or danger where the self is vulnerable (see Point 6) which can guide the therapist in how to think about what might be the core fear driving the client's anxiety.

From the case conceptualization flows the treatment plan and choice of techniques which are likely to be helpful in tackling her anxiety. In this particular case, embarking on a series of graduated 'getting lost' experiments to new places to demonstrate that being lost is often unavoidable and discomforting but time-limited rather than being lost indefinitely – trapped in a traveller's limbo – which emerged from the experiments as the cognitive core of her anxiety, 'I'm going to be lost forever and will never see my family again', and was added to the evolving conceptualization of her problems. The client stated: 'It's utterly ridiculous and I've no idea why I think this. Going to new places further and further away from home increased the chances of becoming a permanently missing person and with all that entails. I can now really understand why getting lost was a truly awful experience for me.' Her new adaptive and pithy response to getting lost was 'Lost, but then found my way again'.

Without a case conceptualization to guide therapy, techniques are likely to be used in a scattershot fashion and the focus of therapy endlessly shifting to what appears to be interesting at any given moment (Blackburn and Twaddle, 1996).

Part 3

CBT PRACTICE

22

SETTING THE SCENE

By setting the scene, we mean not plunging straight into therapy in order to 'get the client better' as quickly as possible but, instead, preparing the ground before the commencement of formal therapy. This involves welcoming the client in a courteous manner and engaging in a little chit-chat to break the ice (e.g. 'How was your journey?'). Clients can be asked if there are any initial questions they want to ask before the therapist starts to elicit their reasons for seeking counselling at the present time (e.g. 'I've had enough. I'll do whatever it takes to sort my life out'; 'I want to see what therapy can offer'; 'I do want to move forward but it's going to mean a lot of upheaval which I'm not sure about'; or 'My wife's putting pressure on me to seek help. I don't think there's a problem'). Such reasons can help the therapist to assess each client's level of motivation to change (e.g., respectively, committed, curious, ambivalent and reluctant) and tailor the discussion to reflect it. For example, outlining a treatment plan for the committed, talking about the process and effectiveness of CBT for the curious, looking at the pros and cons of change for the ambivalent, and examining whether a 'non-problem' (e.g. heavy alcohol use) might have some problematic features (e.g. deteriorating marital relationship) for the reluctant.

The therapist can ask clients about their expectations of therapy, which may vary considerably (e.g. 'You sort me out', 'You're going to explore my childhood and blame my parents for my problems', or 'You're going to pressurize me into doing things I don't want to do'), in order to deal with any misapprehensions they may have which can then lead into a brief description of CBT: looking at the thought–feeling link, taking personal responsibility for change, setting an agenda, obtaining a specific problem focus, establishing clear, concrete and measurable goals, collaborating in problem-solving, carrying out homework tasks and becoming a self-therapist – the ultimate goal of CBT. Client feedback is elicited about the CBT model and then permission is sought to proceed with CBT. Before permission is granted, the person is an applicant seeking help; after it, the person becomes a client who has made an informed choice.

The therapist can also discuss digital voice recordings (DVRs) of sessions and the rationale for them: as a cornerstone of supervision for the therapist in determining the quality of her work; and enhanced and accelerated learning for the client by listening to the DVRs between sessions – he may process information in the session poorly because of, for example, his emotional disturbance, his embarrassment about asking for clarification from the therapist or his preoccupation with how he thinks the therapist sees him (e.g. 'She thinks I'm weak and pathetic'). In our experience, the majority of clients agree to have their sessions recorded and are not inhibited by or worried about the presence of the recorder in the counselling room (it is the therapists who are usually worried about recording sessions because they believe they will be exposed in supervision as incompetent).

The therapist can enquire if the client has been in therapy before (what kind?), and what was helpful (e.g. 'The therapist showed genuine interest in my problems. I really felt like I was cared about') and unhelpful about it (e.g. 'Therapy just seemed to wander everywhere. I felt lost'); and if any therapeutic gains have been maintained (e.g. 'I felt a bit better afterwards but now I'm just as anxious as I ever was. I just gave up trying to change'). The therapist can use this information to help build a productive alliance with her client and flag up potential treatment obstacles (e.g. the client's apparent lack of sustained effort). The issue of confidentiality and its limits needs to be discussed, i.e. who else will know about or have access to information regarding the client's problems (e.g. the therapist's supervisor, the GP who referred the client, other health professionals linked to the client's case). Practical issues like fees, timekeeping, treatment contracts if required, length and frequency of sessions, possible duration of therapy (based on regular progress reviews) are agreed upon.

The foregoing requirements for setting the scene might seem like a lot to do before formal therapy begins but it means that clients have a clearer picture of what lies ahead of them and have made an informed choice about proceeding with therapy; also, it might become clear that CBT is not indicated for this client and he needs to be referred elsewhere.

23

UNDERTAKING AN ASSESSMENT

A CBT assessment collects relevant information about the client's presenting problems and this information is distilled into a case conceptualization (see Point 30). Taylor (2006: 99) suggests that 'a good assessment provides the beginnings of a sound therapeutic relationship'. An initial assessment may take a couple of sessions or more to complete but, in practice, assessment continues throughout therapy to refine the case conceptualization. Assessment is where problems are usually converted into disorders (e.g. major depression, health anxiety, social anxiety, post-traumatic stress disorder) based on diagnostic criteria found in the *Diagnostic and Statistical Manual of Mental Disorders* (DSM), fifth edition (DSM-5, American Psychiatric Association [APA], 2013). We say 'usually' because some clients' problems will not fit easily (or even at all) into a DSM disorder and idiosyncratic conceptualizations will need to be developed (e.g. a client wants to understand why he lacks ambition and then learn how to 'fire myself up to get ahead in life'). There are three areas to cover in an assessment.

1   *A detailed understanding of the presenting problem.* This involves collecting data on the main thoughts, feelings, behaviours, physical reactions related to the presenting problem (depression triggered by the end of a relationship). Measures are used to assess the severity of the client's presenting problems (in this case, depression) and act as a baseline for, among other ways, determining the client's progress in therapy (e.g. are the scores coming down (progress) or going up again (setback or relapse?). Two of the most commonly used measures in CBT are the Beck

Depression Inventory (BDI-II; Beck *et al.*, 1996) and the Beck Anxiety Inventory (BAI; Beck *et al.*, 1988). The BDI is a 21-item self-report inventory which provides a rapid assessment of the severity of the client's depression including the degree of hopelessness experienced and the presence of suicidal ideas. The BAI is a 21-item self-report scale measuring the severity of the client's cognitive and physiological responses to anxiety.

2   *How the problem is being maintained.* This looks at a specific example of the problem in terms of A = antecedents or situations; B = beliefs and thoughts; and C = emotional and behavioural consequences.

(A)	(B)	(C)
At home alone, reflecting on the end of the relationship	'I don't deserve this. Why did he leave me? I can't be happy without him.'	Depressed, hurt and angry. Social withdrawal.

A client's emotions are best understood and most intensely felt in specific, not general, contexts. The ABC model provides a simple but powerful demonstration of the way thought influences and maintains emotion; also, her behavioural response of social withdrawal will strengthen her beliefs and deepen her depression – a vicious cycle of despair. More ABC examples can be collected to determine if there are patterns or themes emerging in the client's thoughts and beliefs (e.g. fear of lifelong unhappiness without him).

3   *A longitudinal perspective.* This seeks to understand how past factors may have contributed to the client's vulnerability in life (e.g. she believes she is worthless without a partner) and its relationship to her present problems. These factors could include a series of failed relationships, poor coping when living alone, depressive episodes, desperation to find new partners, strategies to try and prevent relationships failing such as being submissive and eager to please, sociotropic personality (see Point 7).

Assessment evolves into a case conceptualization as the therapist and client discuss, using the cognitive model, how past and present interact to produce and, crucially, maintain the latter's current difficulties and seek to devise an appropriate treatment plan to tackle her problems and achieve her goals. Beck (2011) suggests educating clients about their emotional disorders such as depression or panic so that their presenting problems can be attributed to the disorder rather than to themselves for being 'defective' or 'mad' (e.g. 'It's a relief to know that my problems are common and I'm not all alone in the world with them').

24

ASSESSING CLIENT SUITABILITY FOR CBT

Safran and Segal (1990) developed a ten-item Suitability for Short-Term Cognitive Therapy Rating Scale by rating clients on a 0–5 scale, where a total score of 0 indicates least suitability and a total score of 50 the greatest suitability for short-term CBT. We now show how these ten items were used to assess the suitability for short-term CBT of a client who presented with several emotional problems related to increased pressures at work following company restructuring.

1   *Accessibility of automatic thoughts.* After an explanation and examples of what automatic thoughts are (see Point 3), is the client able to detect and report them? Yes. (4)
2   *Awareness and differentiation of emotions.* Is the client aware of and can distinguish between, for example, her anger, guilt, shame and depression? Partly: she has difficulty in being aware of and distinguishing between shame and guilt. (3.5)
3   *Acceptance of personal responsibility.* The client did accept personal responsibility for change but said 'I really wouldn't have these problems if it wasn't for my boss'. (3)
4   *Compatibility with the cognitive rationale.* The client understood and generally agreed with the cognitive model, including the importance of carrying out homework assignments. (4)
5   *Alliance potential (in session).* Can the client form a productive working alliance with the therapist? The client took umbrage at some of the therapist's questions (e.g. 'What do you mean how do I make myself angry when my

boss asks me to stay late to finish a project?') which might mean a less than optimum alliance potential. (3.5)

6   *Alliance potential (outside of session)*. Is the client able to form productive, positive relationships in her life? There was a mixed picture on this issue (e.g. she had close relationships with others but these could quickly unravel if she suspected disloyalty or lack of respect). (3)

7   *Chronicity of problems*. How long has the client had the problem? The client admitted to long-term dissatisfactions in life but the specific problem she wanted to focus on was of recent onset. (4)

8   *Security operations*. To what extent might the client engage in behaviour (e.g. avoidance) that keeps her safe in her own mind but prevents her from constructively tackling her problems? The client said she would be willing to 'meet the problem head on'. (5)

9   *Focality*. Is the client able to focus on the problem targeted for discussion? The client was able to do this with only occasional prompting from the therapist to 'keep on track'. (5)

10 *Client optimism/pessimism regarding therapy*. To what extent does the client believe that therapy will be able to help her? The client said she was 'hopeful. I know I've got to sort myself out'. (4)

The client's score was 39, making her very suitable for short-term CBT. Safran and Segal (1990) provide no cut-off point of unsuitability for short-term CBT; they merely state that high ratings indicate a good prognosis for therapy and low ratings indicate a poor prognosis. Westbrook *et al.* (2011: 90) caution that this scale 'should be used as a guide rather than a rigid set of criteria' in assessing client suitability for CBT. The client agreed to ten sessions of therapy with progress reviews every three sessions.

Frank Wills suggests that client suitability criteria focuses on, for example, clients' abilities to access their thoughts and differentiate between their feelings, form therapeutic relationships often resemble … [the criteria] of psychologically healthy people, perhaps giving us cause to wonder if we may only be ministering to the 'worried well'. Perhaps these criteria do give reasonable predictions who will do well with CBT, but they may not be able to tell us much about who *could* do well with CBT. We may only start to get a feel for that after several sessions.

(2012: 103, 105; emphasis in original)

We usually suggest to clients unsure about CBT to have several trial sessions before they reach a decision about its applicability to them and their difficulties.

25

STRUCTURING THE THERAPY SESSION

This means that each therapy session, following on from the assessment of the client's problems (see Point 23), will follow a predictable pattern. This pattern is explained to the client as part of his continuing socialization into CBT (see Point 22). The therapist can say something like this:

> I want to find out how your anxiety has been since the last session and look at your scores on the Beck Anxiety Inventory. Is there anything that may have happened during the past week you want to bring up? I'd be interested in any feedback you have from the previous session. Then we can set the agenda so the session remains problem-focused. Okay?

These pre-agenda setting items should be kept to a brief discussion (no more than a maximum of ten minutes) as the main focus of the session is working through the agenda. The therapist can encourage the client to be succinct in his replies to these items by asking very specific questions such as, 'Has there been any improvement in your sleep pattern in the last week?' rather than 'How have you been feeling in the last week?' which can result in a lot of detail not relevant to the client's problem. If an issue does emerge that either the client or therapist wants to explore further (e.g. the client says that therapy is not helping him), then this issue can be put on the agenda, not discussed independently of it. If the client expresses any suicidal ideas, these become the immediate agenda.

Structuring the session is a skilful and disciplined procedure to carry out and, in our experience, therapists, both novice and experienced, often neglect to do it in their eagerness to 'get at' the client's problem or because of their unease at placing a 'straitjacket' on the session (in the latter case, the session is usually unproductive if discussion is diffuse instead of focused).

26

SETTING THE AGENDA

An agenda is a short list of items that will be the focus of that particular session. Setting an agenda is deemed by cognitive behaviour therapists to be the best way of making the optimum use of the therapy time (though clients who have been in non-directive forms of therapy may become irritated at what they see as restrictions on their freedom to wander mentally; the therapist may need to explain patiently and repeatedly the rationale for agenda setting). The agenda items are jointly agreed though reviewing and negotiating homework tasks are permanent fixtures on the agenda. A typical agenda looks like this:

- Reviewing homework – what learning did the client extract from carrying out his homework assignment? (See Point 66.)
- Working on the client's prioritized problems and the key cognitions and behaviours connected to them. Clients are encouraged to be succinct in discussing their difficulties so therapy does not get bogged down in long-winded storytelling detail.
- Negotiating new homework – what goal-relevant assignment does the client want to execute in the next week? (See Point 65.)
- Summarizing the session – initially, this is usually done by the therapist but is gradually transferred to the client as he gains competence and confidence in his developing role as a self-therapist.
- Feedback – what did the client find helpful and unhelpful about today's session? The client's reply to that last question should be greeted non-defensively by the therapist.

The last three items can take from 10–15 minutes to complete so it is important that the therapist keeps an eye on the time to prevent the session overrunning or the squeezing of these items into the few remaining minutes of the session.

27

DRAWING UP A PROBLEM LIST

Clients usually present with more than one problem. The list can be 'ticked off' as progress is made on each problem. A problem list is drawn up in the initial stages of assessment but is not fixed for the remainder of therapy: problems can be added to or deleted from the list. Problems are prioritized in terms of the expected progress to be made tackling them within the allotted time for therapy (e.g. eight sessions). Additionally, the problems and their resolution are stated in clear and concrete terms that allow for progress to be regularly measured, and the interventions used to treat these problems have, where possible, an evidence base of proven effectiveness (Wills, 2012).

Sometimes a client will present with a large number of problems that can leave both client and therapist feeling overwhelmed. I (MN) once saw a client who read out her problems from a notebook – the final count was 53! However, it quickly became apparent as I was listening to her that her anxiety in these situations was linked to a fear of incurring the disapproval of significant others in her life, particularly those she saw as socially and intellectually superior to her, which would then activate her core belief that she was inferior for having a poor education and working-class upbringing (she agreed with my hypothesis). It is important for the therapist to be able to pinpoint the beliefs and behaviours that connect seemingly disparate problems in order to develop a simple case conceptualization – not a prolix one – which then helps both client and therapist to see clearly these key cognitive and behavioural factors maintaining the client's various problems (see Point 30). As Fennell observes:

The problem list … imposes order on chaos. A mass of distressing experiences is reduced to a number of relatively specific difficulties. This process of 'problem-reduction' is crucial to the encouragement of hope, since it implies the possibility of control.

(1989: 179)

28

AGREEING ON GOALS

We say 'agreeing on goals' because the therapist does not automatically go along with the client's goal selection. The client might select a goal that is outside of her control (e.g. 'I want my husband to come back to me'), counterproductive (e.g. 'I want to feel nothing when people hurt or criticize me') or unrealistic (e.g. 'I never want to ever experience another panic attack'). For each problem on the list there will be a specific goal. Wells advises that

> Once problems have been prioritised they should be *reframed* as goals. The problem list provides details of *'what is wrong'* and this should be changed into a goal or a statement of *'what the patient would like to happen'*. Goals should be *operationalised* [made therapeutically useful] in concrete terms.
>
> (1997: 51; italics in original)

Clients are prone to state their goals in vague (e.g. 'I want to feel less disconnected from myself') or general terms (e.g. 'I want to be happy in life'). The therapist would need to ask each client what specific changes would have to occur in order for these goals to be operationalized (e.g., respectively, 'I want to be more assertive at home in speaking up for myself' and 'I want to be in a relationship'). The next step is to decide how progress towards these specific goals can be assessed or measured (e.g., respectively, keeping a diary recording her assertiveness at home, and joining a dating service and going on dates – not always the same thing as some clients do not get beyond the joining stage). Derived from the world of business management, clients can engage in SMART goal-setting.

Specific – 'I want to be able to go from my house to the high street on my own.'

Measurable – currently housebound and can only leave the house if accompanied by a family member or friend. House to high street progress can be assessed in stages.

Achievable – the client believes she has the ability and determination to carry out the goal-oriented action plan.

Realistic – the client states that her goal is rooted in reality, not a flight of fancy or a dream that is out of reach.

Timescale – this goal seems achievable within the time the client has allotted to stay in therapy.

Dobson and Dobson (2009) suggest that the SMART model is best suited for behavioural goals though any goal can be subjected to SMART criteria. Goals should be stated in positive terms (e.g. 'I want to eventually feel calmer and more confident when making presentations to groups') instead of negative terms (e.g. 'I don't want to feel so anxious and awkward when talking to a group of people') so 'that it is explicit what the patient is moving *towards* rather than away from' (Kirk, 1989: 41; emphasis in original). Additionally, goal-setting 'reinforces the notion that the patient is an active member of the therapeutic relationship, and that full involvement is required: the patient will not be "done" to' (Kirk, 1989: 41). Goals are flexible, not fixed, and can change in the light of incoming information (e.g. from homework assignments) that the client's initial goal was too ambitious, given the long-standing nature of her problems, or that she wants to capitalize on the unexpected quick progress she is making by now selecting a more challenging goal.

29

TEACHING THE COGNITIVE MODEL

During the first session of CBT it is important for the therapist to orient her clients to the thought–feeling link; in other words, to teach the cognitive model. The therapist's clinical judgement can determine the best time or moment to introduce the model. For example, the client might attend the appointment in an anxious state and it may be productive for the therapist to elicit there and then her client's anxiety-provoking thinking: 'What thoughts are going through your mind right now to make you anxious about coming here?' The client might reply: 'I'm worried you're not going to be able to help me and I'll never get better.' The therapist can ask her client what thoughts would reduce his anxiety: 'I suppose if I thought you could help me and there was hope for me after all.'

During the session the client might fall silent, become tearful, react angrily to a question, or stare at the floor. Such moments can become opportunities for teaching the model by exploring the client's thinking with a 'What's going through your mind right now to make you tearful?' type question. Writing the thought–feeling link on a whiteboard or flipchart can help the client in two ways: to step back from his upsetting thoughts and feelings in order to examine them more objectively; and make the cognitive model more concrete, vivid and understandable. The above examples are meant to teach the model through the use of questions so that the client makes the thought–feeling connection himself rather than being told by the therapist.

However, the therapist can take a didactic stance in teaching the model. You feel the way you think (Burns, 1999) might be the starting point: 'Let me explain what I mean by that statement by giving you an example. Two men are very keen on the same woman. They both ask her out and she rejects both of them. Now it's the same situation for both of them, rejection, but one man becomes depressed because he tells himself he's not attractive and no woman will ever want him while the other man is disappointed because he tells himself it's unfortunate he didn't get to go out with her but it's no big deal to be rejected. It's not the situation that makes each man feel the way that he does, but how each man interprets the situation that influences how he feels. That is the essence of the model: you feel the way you think.' The therapist can then show her client how the model can be used to understand his emotional reactions to life events, e.g. the client says he is anxious in social situations because he fears people will find him boring and avoid him. As Blackburn and Davidson point out:

> The therapist would indicate how the interpretation was congruent with the feeling but not necessarily the only interpretation possible. Such examples from the patient's own experiences would lead the therapist to demonstrate how cognitive therapy is relevant for the individual and might help to overcome his dysphoric moods.
>
> (1995: 56)

It is important for the therapist to remember that the client might understand the model but not agree with it (the mistake is to assume understanding for agreement); therefore, any reservations about or objections to the model need to be elicited (e.g. 'The model doesn't make any sense if you're in a concentration camp or dying of a terminal illness, does it?') and addressed (see Point 1 for example). The client does not need to have complete conviction in the model to benefit from therapy: he can make progress despite some doubts about the model's applicability to every situation in his life. Teaching the cognitive model is not a 'one off' but is done frequently throughout the course of therapy, with the client taking increasing responsibility for making his thought–feelings links and demonstrating to himself that by changing his upsetting thinking he is able to ameliorate his unpleasant moods. Therefore for many clients, taking responsibility for their emotional reactions to events is a liberating rather than an unwelcome message because it shows them that they do not have to rely on changing others or situations first before they can feel better which, if this was the case, would make personal change very much more difficult to achieve.

30

DEVELOPING A CASE CONCEPTUALIZATION

This means making sense of the client's problems within the cognitive behavioural model of emotional disorders (to what extent is the model compatible with the client's view of the development and maintenance of his problems?). Westbrook *et al.* (2011) suggest a case conceptualization (or formulation) consists of three components:

1 a description of the current problem(s);
2 an account of why and how these problems might have developed;
3 an analysis of the key maintaining processes hypothesized to perpetuate the problems.

These three components can be tied together in the following example: a client who presents with major depression triggered by the end of a relationship (e.g. 'Why did he dump me for her? My life is meaningless without him. What did I do to drive him away? I can't face seeing anyone without him') may point to underlying intermediate beliefs (e.g. 'Unless I'm in a relationship, my life has no meaning') and core beliefs (e.g. 'I'm nobody on my own') which are long-standing cognitive vulnerability factors activated by the current stressors in the client's life (see Appendix 1 for an example of case conceptualization).

Butler *et al.* (2008) advance three key principles which guide case conceptualization:

1   A conceptualization should be based on attempting to translate theory into practice (see the first sentence at the top of the page).
2   A conceptualization should be hypothetical, i.e. both therapist and client are able to confirm, modify or discount the data used in developing one.
3   The conceptualization should be parsimonious (concise and clear). The more complex and verbose the conceptualization, the harder it will be to remember and use for both therapist and client.

The case conceptualization serves as the basis for a treatment plan: the client may wish to learn how to be relatively happy and independent by living on her own in order to give meaning to her life in the absence of a relationship and learning that she will always be a somebody whether or not she is in a relationship; the homework assignments will be directed towards achieving these goals. Without the conceptualization, techniques and interventions are likely to be used in a 'hit or miss' way because the therapist has rushed into treatment based on a cursory understanding of the client's problems, e.g. 'She needs a behavioural activation programme of going on some dates and more socializing to lift her mood.'

A tentative case conceptualization is started in the first session and is continually refined/modified in the light of new information until therapy is terminated. Wills and Sanders (1997) suggest that a good case conceptualization helps the client to answer such questions as 'Why me?', 'Why now?', 'Why doesn't the problem go away?' and 'How do I get better?' The therapist shares the conceptualization with his client to determine its accuracy as well as to help the client understand herself and her problems better (Beck, 2011).

As we said in Point 23, problems, where possible, are converted into disorders based on DSM-5 diagnostic criteria and while 'diagnoses are important for beginning to build a case formulation and treatment plan ... diagnoses are insufficient in themselves for this purpose' (Taylor, 2006: 99). The reason they are insufficient is because the client's particular presentation of the disorder needs to be understood. For example, two clients get the same diagnosis of social anxiety disorder and therefore appear to have identical problems; however, a case conceptualization for each client reveals that the first client has poor social skills (e.g. passivity, difficulties in initiating and sustaining conversations) while the second one has good social skills but these are impaired by anxiety in certain situations. While treatment for both clients will be similar in certain respects, the first client would receive social skills training which would not be necessary for the second one.

A recent addition to case conceptualization is listings clients' strengths (to balance their perceived weaknesses) which can be used in tackling their current difficulties: 'A primary purpose of case conceptualization is building client resilience' (Kuyken *et al.*, 2009: 55). These authors suggest that for some clients case conceptualization is less likely to be overwhelming or distressing if the focus is as much on what is right with them as it is on what is wrong with them. Sometimes resilience itself can be the framework within which a client's problem are understood and tackled (Neenan, 2009), e.g. 'I want to learn to be more resilient when faced with setbacks and upsets in my life instead of continually overreacting to them.'

Even though a case conceptualization is supposed to be straightforward to understand, some clients might still find it difficult to grasp or want a concise and vivid way of capturing their problems; in these cases, the therapist and client can construct a capsule conceptualization: summing up in a memorable single sentence the problem and the proposed solution to it. For example:

- Blowing away the cobwebs – the client at long last examines some of his long-held beliefs and realises they have long outlived their usefulness as they do not reflect the changes his life has actually undergone: people do not punish him for disagreeing with them like his parents did many years ago. He now focuses on developing new adaptive beliefs that take into account these changes.

- Crossing the Rubicon – this time, there is no giving up or going back and the client will persevere until her goal is achieved of leaving an abusive relationship.
- Waking up the sleeping dogs – the days of unassertiveness are coming to an end and the client will now start standing up for himself and his interests when he believes he is being unfairly treated by some friends and work colleagues.
- Breaking the spell – a client finally faces the unpleasant reality that her 'dream man' is never going to leave his wife in order to create the perfect relationship with her, and sadly concludes she is wasting her life with her unrequited devotion to him and it is time to move on.

31

DEVELOPING TREATMENT PLANS

A treatment plan is derived from the client's case conceptualization and provides an overall view of how the client can free himself from the 'grip' of the disorder and achieve his therapy goals. The treatment plan is composed of a series of interventions that will modify those factors maintaining the client's disorder (if a client objects to the term 'treatment plan' as it sounds too medical, the therapist can substitute 'action plan'). Treatment usually comes in the form of research-based disorder-specific treatment manuals (e.g. for post-traumatic stress disorder [PTSD] which provides structure for each session and guides the therapist in which procedures and techniques to use. The advice for using these manuals is fidelity with flexibility, i.e. these interventions have been shown to work from clinical trials so stick with them, but not rigidly; the therapist has to tailor the treatment plan to the concerns and requirements of individual clients as revealed in their case conceptualizations.

Before we look at a treatment plan for panic disorder, what is the cognitive model of panic? It is when

> individuals experience panic attacks because they have a relatively enduring tendency to interpret a range of bodily sensations [e.g. racing heart, breathlessness, feeling unreal] in a catastrophic fashion … [this] catastrophic misinterpretation involves perceiving these sensations as indicative of an *immediately* impending physical or mental disaster [a racing heart will result in a heart attack; breathlessness will lead to suffocation; and feeling unreal means going crazy].
>
> (Clark, 1989: 57; emphasis in original)

The treatment programme derived from this model has been empirically validated (Clark, 1996) and aims to help clients change their interpretations of bodily sensations from catastrophic to benign and modify the processes that maintain these catastrophic interpretations. Cognitive interventions include teaching clients the cognitive model of panic, examining the evidence for their catastrophic interpretations (e.g. 'My heart was banging so loud. It can't possibly stand the strain of that'; 'I couldn't get my breath. The pressure in my chest was so tight'); then examining the evidence for alternative, benign explanations of their bodily symptoms (e.g. 'When you're anxious, your heart rate speeds up. Your heart was designed to deal with a great deal of stress and strain without damaging itself'; 'Breathlessness is caused by over-breathing; it does not mean you're suffocating. You always get air no matter how bad you feel').

Behavioural interventions include therapist-guided in-session panic induction (inducing feared bodily sensations by, for example, running on the spot for several minutes or deliberately hyper-ventilating) in order to teach clients that their very unpleasant panic sensations are not dangerous; and later in therapy, clients visit avoided situations alone and induce their feared sensations in these feared situations, e.g. a client getting his heart to race by running up several flights of stairs in a department store in order to demonstrate to himself that a heart attack will not occur.

Does this treatment programme produce a successful outcome for clients? Clark states that 'controlled trials indicate that this specialized form of cognitive therapy is a specific, and highly effective, treatment for panic disorder' (1996: 339); i.e. the majority of clients at the end of treatment are, and remain at follow-up, panic free. Treatment plans for depression and anxiety disorders can be found in Leahy *et al.* (2012).

32

DETECTING NATS

As we discussed in Point 3, NATs are situation-specific thoughts that usually lie on the fringes of awareness. Some clients can report their NATs without any prompting from the therapist while other clients may be 'completely unaware of them; they are so much a part of his view of himself and the world that they do not appear distorted or problematic' (Persons, 1989: 116). Clients are often more aware of how they feel (e.g. 'I was terribly irritable all morning') than the thoughts connected to the feelings (e.g. 'I can't put my finger on why I was feeling like that'). NATs are the first type of thoughts that clients are taught to examine as they are the easiest to detect and modify. This does not mean that clients will offer only NATs when revealing their situation-specific upsetting thinking: underlying assumptions and core beliefs are likely to be uncovered too. The therapist needs to 'sort through' this cognitive data in order to categorize it.

The therapist can normalize NATs by helping clients to see that everyone experiences them and they often 'pop up' when we feel upset. Often these thoughts are dismissed, challenged or ignored. However, difficulties with NATs start when they are linked to prolonged emotional distress, are difficult to 'turn off', not submitted to rational reflection or empirical testing, seem plausible to the person and reflect the content of activated core beliefs (e.g. 'I'm a failure').

While we emphasize detecting NATs, clients can also experience self-defeating PATs (positive automatic thoughts). Some examples: a person with a past history of alcohol abuse decides to start drinking again (e.g. 'A couple of drinks won't hurt. I'll feel great. I deserve a treat. Yeah, go for it!'); a person with bulimia nervosa convinces herself that she can eat what she wants because 'I won't gain weight as I'll make myself sick afterwards' (Cooper *et al.*, 2000). These kinds of PATs also need to be detected, examined and modified.

In this point and the following ones (33–48), we look at some of the main ways of detecting NATs. Asking direct questions is the most straightforward way of eliciting NATs. For example: 'Do you know what was going through your mind at that moment to make you so nervous when your boss asked you take over an important project?' This approach can quickly establish if the client has the ability, at the present time, to detect such thoughts. The client's introspection can be aided by the therapist's clear and specific questions (as above) instead of vague and rambling ones (e.g. 'In that situation where you were getting nervous, you know the situation with your boss, what do you think you were thinking when your boss asked you to take over the project that led you to be so nervous based on what you were thinking about when he asked you?').

Evocative questions can 'prise loose' some NATs when a client has responded with 'I don't know' to initial enquiries. For example, when a client says he does not know what goes through his mind to make him very anxious when he is the centre of attention, the therapist asks: 'What thoughts go through your mind at that very moment when all eyes are on you, *scrutinizing* you, *judging* you?' The client, who was now visibly anxious, replied: 'They'll see me as a fat, undisciplined slob and despise me.' The therapist's evocative question was based on a hypothesis she had developed from information collected during the assessment of the client's problems.

With a client who is completely unaware of his NATs because they are a natural part of his world view (Persons, 1989), questions can help to reveal them by the client imagining himself not acting in accordance with his world view. For example, a client says that he puts himself at the back of any queue in life – 'That's just the way I am'. The therapist asks: 'Just imagine putting yourself at the front of the queue for a change. What thoughts would be going through your mind if you did that?' The client's reply reveals his NATs: 'I would be selfish for doing that. It would mean that my needs are more important than other people's in the queue. I'd be getting above myself. I don't deserve to put myself first in the queue.'

33

GUIDED DISCOVERY

Guided discovery is a process whereby the therapist acts as a guide to help clients: uncover, examine and reality-test their maladaptive thoughts and beliefs; develop adaptive and balanced responses to these cognitions; and make better problem-solving decisions. A method of guided discovery is Socratic questioning derived from the Greek philosopher Socrates (*c.* 469–399 BC):

> If Socrates thought he could lead his interlocutors [those engaged in debate with him] to the truth by his questioning, it was because he believed that the truth is already in us, albeit often unknown to us … so when we learn the truth we are not really learning it, but remembering what we once knew and have forgotten.
>
> (Kolakowski, 2008: 4-5)

Based on the information revealed through Socratic questioning, clients will often say something like, 'I knew that already but I seem to have it lost somewhere'. Socratic questioning is driven by the therapist's genuine curiosity to understand the client's viewpoint, not a manufactured curiosity that wearily assumes he is going to hear all the expected answers. Beck *et al.* point out that 'questions should be phrased in such a way that they stimulate thought and increase awareness, rather than requiring a correct answer' (1993: 103), e.g. respectively, 'Do you know why you take criticism so badly?' versus 'Criticism makes you believe you're inferior, doesn't it?' Also, guided discovery through Socratic questioning enables the client to provide her own answers rather than rely on the interpretations that might be offered by the therapist which can put the client 'in a compromising position – in that it is simpler to agree than to disagree, or to seem ungrateful or difficult' (Blackburn and Twaddle, 1996: 8–9). If the client does believe she is in a 'compromising position' she may be reluctant to reveal additional thoughts that might be more pertinent to understanding her problems.

As Socratic questioning requires clients to think about their answers, the therapist should be wary about responding too quickly to the client's seeming inability or struggle to answer the question as premature intervention 'interrupts the client's thought processes and disrupts the purpose of the Socratic question' (DiGiuseppe, 1991a: 184). In our experience, responding too quickly is often based on the therapist's awkwardness with protracted silences or her impatience with the client's slowness in 'moving therapy along' which might then indicate therapist incompetence. In the following example, the therapist uses guided discovery in order to uncover the client's NATs:

Client: I'm sitting at home the other night, looking out the window at the rain and I started to feel really depressed. I don't know what was going on with me to feel like that.

Therapist: Shall we see if we can find out? [client nods] Can you remember what you were thinking as you were looking at the rain?

Client: Just that it was a horrible night to be out and about.

Therapist: Were you glad to be in then?

Client: Yes, on that night but I always seem to stay in.

Therapist: How come you 'always seem to stay in'?

Client: Because I've got nowhere to go, no one to see. [client's mood drops and she stares at the floor]

Therapist: What does it mean to you that you've 'got nowhere to go, no one to see'?

Client: That my life is dull and boring. I'm drifting along with no future, no prospect of happiness.

Therapist: Are those the thoughts [NATs] that brought on the depression? [client nods]

Padesky and Greenberger (1995) call guided discovery 'a cornerstone of cognitive therapy', and it takes a lot of practice to be proficient in its use. However, do not persevere unproductively with Socratic questioning (which could turn into 'mental torture' accompanied by a string of exasperated 'I don't know!' replies from the client) if it becomes obvious that the client would clearly benefit from direct explanations of how to solve his problems. Once this is done, the therapist can return to a Socratic style by asking the client for his comments on the proposed solution. As well as Socratic questioning, another method of guided discovery is behavioural experiments (see Point 59).

34

USING IMAGERY

The term 'cognition' includes images as well as thoughts. Some clients might find it difficult to pinpoint their NATs in a specific situation, but the therapist can ask such clients if they had any pictures or images in their minds in that situation which might be more retrievable (e.g. 'I had an image of everyone turning their backs on me when I entered the room'). Then the client, in this example, can be asked what meaning he attaches to the image in order to elicit his accompanying thoughts (e.g. 'I've lost their respect and I'll never get it back'). Using imagery can help clients to relive past situations in order to uncover the hot (emotionally charged) thoughts associated with these situations. For example, a client who said she felt anxious when walking in the high street, but did not know why, was asked to imagine the situation in the present tense, as if it was happening right now:

Client: I'm walking down the high street. I feel very uncomfortable. I think everyone is looking at me, so I keep my head down.

Therapist: What would you be seeing if you put your head up?

Client: I always keep it down and just rush about to get my shopping over with as quickly as possible.

Therapist: But imagine putting your head up and looking around. What do you see?

Client: [becoming visibly tense] I see them staring at me, judging me. I hate it.

Therapist: What is it that they are judging?

Client: [becoming tearful] My looks.

Therapist: In what way?

Client: They think I'm ugly, hideous. I look like the elephant woman. They probably make jokes about me and have a good laugh. I can't bear it.

Therapist: Are those the thoughts that make you so anxious when you go into the high street?

Client: [quietly] Yes.

Lazarus states that an 'understanding of the role that imagery plays in our daily lives provides a clue to unraveling otherwise insoluble puzzles' (1984: 20). Such a puzzle is when a client presents with a situation that he says he should be very happy about (e.g. getting married) but, instead, feels worried and standard CBT questioning fails to elucidate his worry. To bring the client's worries into focus, the therapist can use the step-up technique (Lazarus, 1984) where the client visualizes his married life unfolding and the therapist keeps 'stepping up' the image (moving forward in time) to the point where the worrying thoughts emerge: 'I can see it in my mind's eye now. Her irritating habits have become intolerable. I resent her more than I love her, but she'll be destroyed if I leave her. So I'm trapped in the marriage and feel very unhappy.'

MAKING SUGGESTIONS

No matter how skilful the therapist is as a Socratic questioner (see Point 33), there usually comes a point in therapy when the client responds with 'I don't know' and further questions from the therapist do not help the client to find ways of overcoming his cognitive block. In order to tackle this block, the therapist can make some suggestions based on the client's case conceptualization or derived from her clinical experience. In the following example, a client says 'I really have no idea why I feel so guilty if I spend time just reading a newspaper or watching television':

Therapist: [reading from the conceptualization] One of your underlying assumptions is 'If I don't have a real job then I'm not as good as others'. Now you've been out of work for several years due to illness and you said you try to cram a lot of activity into each day to prove that you are as good as others by having a job at home, so to speak; so do you see reading the newspaper or watching television as an indulgence, idling when you should be striving?

Client: Yes, that's exactly it now that you've mentioned it. It is an indulgence. I should be working hard to make up for not having a real job. I don't deserve any time to myself. I feel a failure if I don't complete my daily to-do lists. (The last four sentences are the client's NATs.)

In this example, a suggestion from the therapist provided the stimulus for productive introspection on the client's part; it would have been unproductive on the therapist's part to make further suggestions when the client was not in need of them (a surfeit of suggestions can help to induce passivity in a client as the therapist does most of her thinking for her). If the client had agreed with the therapist that she was indulging herself but provided no elaboration on her agreement, then the therapist could have asked: 'How does this indulgence lead you to feel guilty?' Such a question is designed to assess whether the client is being compliant with the therapist's suggestion (e.g. 'I was only agreeing with you. I don't want to appear difficult') or whether the suggestion has been genuinely helpful to the client in providing answers to her bafflement.

Another way of stimulating a client's introspection when he becomes stymied in pinpointing his situation-specific automatic thoughts is for the therapist to suggest a thought opposite to the client's expected response (Beck, 2011). For example, the client is uncertain why he feels so anxious about being asked out by a very attractive woman. The therapist says: 'You're anxious because you believe that she will see you as the perfect man for her.' The client replies: 'On the contrary. I think I'll disappoint her both in and out of bed. I won't live up to expectations (NATs).' The therapist can then tease out through Socratic questioning why the client thinks he will disappoint her and whose expectations he will not live up to – his own or what he imagines are her expectations of him.

36

IN-SESSION EMOTIONAL CHANGES

Changes in a client's emotional state can occur at any point in each session. The therapist needs to be alert to these emotional shifts as they are important entry points into the client's thinking. These shifts can be obvious (e.g. becoming angry) or subtle (e.g. narrowing eyes). The client may be talking about an issue in a non-emotive way when the therapist notices something in his manner that she infers is an emotional change:

Therapist: That was quite a sigh. How are you feeling at this moment?

Client: Down.

Therapist: What thoughts are going through your mind right now to make you feel down?

Client: I've let so many things slip through my fingers. What a waste. Why didn't I grasp these opportunities and make the most of them?

Encouraging the client to answer his own question will help to make explicit the meaning implied by the question. Beck *et al.* stress the importance of ascertaining the meanings in clients' communications:

The *totality* of the meaning of the patient's experience is crucial. At times, the meanings people give to a situation may not be fully formulated but rather will have to be drawn out by the therapist ... by relying exclusively on the immediate raw data of the automatic thoughts, the therapist misses the crucial – but unexpressed – meaning.

(1979: 30; emphasis in original)

The meaning of the client's last automatic thought is now ascertained by the therapist:

Therapist: What's your answer to your own question?

Client: I don't have the guts to succeed. I'll never amount to anything important in life. My life is an endless catalogue of missed opportunities. [client becomes tearful and stares at the floor slowly shaking his head]

The client's answer is filled with 'hot thoughts'. These are thoughts 'that are most connected to moods ... [and] conduct the emotional charge' (Greenberger and Padesky, 1995: 55), and are the most important NATs to elicit and modify. CBT is not interested in NATs *per se* because many of them will be peripheral or irrelevant to the understanding of the client's emotional reactions in certain contexts; so therapists may need to comb through a number of NATs in order to pinpoint collaboratively the 'hot' ones (see Point 46). By encouraging clients to imagine vividly the problematic situation as if it is happening right now often accelerates the discovery of 'hot' NATs.

37

FINDING THE THOUGHTS BY ASCERTAINING THE CLIENT'S IDIOSYNCRATIC MEANING OF THE EVENT

Blackburn and Davidson point out that 'patients often talk about events as if they were the cause of their bad feelings. The therapist establishes the missing link (the interpretation) by *ascertaining the meaning of the event*' (1995: 73; emphasis in original). In the following example, the client believes the situation made him feel guilty:

Situation	Emotion
Arriving ten minutes late to pick up his sons from school	Guilty

The client supports his viewpoint by stating that if he got to the school on time then he would not have felt guilty, so 'it surely follows that the situation made me feel guilty because I turned up late'. In response to the therapist's enquiry, the client tentatively agrees that not every father (or parent) would feel guilty if he arrived late at the school to pick up his children. Having made this opening into his thinking, the therapist asks him what it means to him to turn up late at the school:

Situation	Thoughts	Emotion
Arriving ten minutes late to pick up his sons from school	My boys were very worried when I wasn't there to pick them up. I shouldn't have worried them like that. I'm a bad father for putting them through such an ordeal.	Guilty

Thus the therapist demonstrates to the client that his feelings are mediated by his interpretation of the situation and not directly caused by the situation itself. The client replies: 'It makes sense. If I had arrived late and my boys were playing about enjoying themselves, then I would have felt relieved, not guilty.' The therapist writing the situation-thoughts-feelings sequence on a whiteboard or flipchart in the counselling room can help the client to gain greater objectivity in seeing the crucial role cognitions play in powerfully influencing his emotional reactions to events.

Some thought record forms used in CBT put the emotion column after the situation column and before the thoughts column. This seems very strange to us and we agree with Dobson and Dobson (2009) that these particular forms are inconsistent with the cognitive model of emotional disorders as they give the impression that situations cause emotions; putting thoughts between the situation and emotion columns is consistent with the model; namely, our emotional responses to events are mediated by our thinking about these events.

38

FOCUSING ON FEELINGS

Beck has called emotion 'the royal road [short and easy way] to cognition' (quoted in Padesky, 1993a: 404), and helping clients to activate and explore their feelings usually reveals important NATs. For example, a client who says he feels angry about his father's behaviour towards him but is reluctant to tell him is encouraged by the therapist to imagine that his father is sitting opposite him in the counselling room and to 'tell him how you're feeling':

Client: [talking to his father] I'm angry with you. I asked you out for a drink last Sunday and you said you were too busy. Why are you always too busy when I try and arrange something for us to do together? I feel you're always pushing me away from you. Why do you do this to me?

Therapist: Why do you think your father is always pushing you away?

Client: [becoming tearful] He doesn't love me. I'll never be good enough for him unlike my brother. He'd disown me if he could. Nothing I do ever pleases him. [hot thoughts]

The use of chairwork, as shown above, is usually associated with Gestalt therapy, not CBT. Cognitive behaviour therapists borrow techniques from other therapeutic approaches, but these techniques are used within the framework of the cognitive model of emotional disorders (Clark and Steer, 1996) – in the above example, to elicit hot thoughts.

Clients can keep a mood diary and note changes in mood in order to 'catch' their NATs. Michael Free likens catching NATs to hunting a very shy animal:

> We have to find out about the AT's [automatic thoughts] habits. We can look for its tracks or droppings. With automatic thoughts we can tell where they've been by the emotion they leave behind … a stab of anxiety, a brief sinking feeling, a flash of anger. Be on the lookout for those signs and see if you can catch a glimpse of the automatic thoughts. As you get used to it you will be able to see more of the AT, until you are able to write it down in a complete sentence.
>
> (1999: 61)

For example, a client keeps a mood diary and notes momentary panics when she is asked by her boss to undertake impromptu tasks and 'glimpses' part of the automatic thought, 'Oh God!' Through regular recording in her diary of these panics, and thereby becoming accustomed to them rather than startled by them, she is eventually able to see the full automatic thought(s): 'Oh God! I've got to use my initiative. I'll make a mess of things. My boss will think I'm really incompetent and regret promoting me.'

If a client presents with an emotionally impoverished vocabulary (e.g. uses the word 'bad' to describe all his feelings), the therapist can provide information to widen his perspective on emotional responses to events:

> For example, there's bad depression where we might see ourselves as a failure and withdraw from others; bad guilt by doing something we should or shouldn't have done and seeing ourselves as a horrible person for this out of character behaviour; bad hurt when we believe we've been let down by others and don't deserve it and we sulk about it; there's bad shame about our inadequacies being exposed to others and therefore not wanting to look people in the eyes or avoiding them. Any of those bad experiences ring a bell with you?

The client said he felt 'bad hurt' as his wife had an affair when he was working all hours 'to put food on the table for the family' and he did not deserve this 'betrayal, so why should I talk to her when she's done this to me?'

39

ASSUMING THE WORST

Wells states that 'one of the most effective questions for eliciting NATs in the therapeutic dialogue is *"What's the worst that could happen if …"* ' (1997: 58; emphasis in original). Freeman *et al.* (1993) suggest that this question should not be asked unless the therapist believes that the client is capable of: understanding the hypothetical nature of the question, developing adaptive responses to highly adverse events, and benefiting from the idea that 'If I can handle the worst, then I can handle anything else less than the worst'. Additionally, this question is indicated if the worst outcome is based on a highly distorted reading of future events such as 'My whole life will be totally ruined if I fail the exam' or 'I'll be so terrified of the plane crashing I'll be running up and down the aisles screaming and vomiting over everyone'. In the following example, a client with performance anxiety is asked to consider the worst.

Client: I'll give a terrible performance.

Therapist: That's a general description of your performance. What specific aspects of it are you most anxious about?

Client: I'll be so nervous talking to all those people that I'll become tongue-tied.

Therapist: What's the worst that could happen if you become tongue-tied?

Client: I'll freeze, nothing will come out of my mouth.

Therapist: Is that the worst that could happen?

Client: No. The worst thing is that I'll be exposed as a phoney, a nervous wreck, and my professional credibility will be destroyed. [the client's key NATs or hottest thoughts have been identified]

Assuming the worst can also be undertaken if the client's imagined fear could occur and he wants to face it (e.g. terminal illness, the end of a long-standing relationship); or if the client avoids focusing on it directly but it continually distracts him in therapy which the therapist points out: 'You say you're worried about your son's strange behaviour because you believe he's overfriendly with another man, but it seems to me that what you're most worried about is that your son may be gay, the unspoken but nagging subject in therapy. Is there any truth in what I've said?'

40

SITUATIONAL EXPOSURE

Situational exposure occurs when clients agree to face the feared situations they usually avoid in order to elicit their hot thoughts. In the safety of the counselling room the client may find it difficult to gain access to such thoughts because he is obviously not in the situation which triggers them, he may play down the distressing nature of the thoughts (e.g. 'I'm being silly really. I know nothing really bad is going to happen to me'), or he may have thought something 'terrible' was going to happen and quickly left the situation but now cannot specify what the terrible event was that he believed would occur. By encouraging clients to enter into feared or avoided situations, their hot thoughts can be activated. For example, a client who is afraid of eating in public but cannot say why is accompanied to a local café by the therapist.

Client:	I feel everyone's looking at me while I eat. I feel so tense and hot, my throat's dry. It's hard to chew and swallow my food.
Therapist:	What do you think is going to happen if you stay here and continue to eat?
Client:	I'm going to embarrass myself.
Therapist:	In what way?
Client:	I'll get so tense. I won't be able to get the food down and I'll start to choke on it. Then I'll spit it out or it will dribble out of my mouth. I'll make an awful spectacle of myself. People will be appalled at my behaviour and turn away in disgust. (The last four thoughts are the key NATs.)

This exposure to a previously avoided situation yielded crucial assessment data that remained untapped while the client was sitting in the therapist's office. Accompanying clients on such trips early in therapy is often necessary as they are hardly likely at this stage to carry out such feared trips alone in order to record their thoughts.

ROLE PLAY

This is used when clients have difficulty revealing key thoughts in their problematic relations with others. The therapist can play the person with whom the client experiences interpersonal difficulties. It is important that the therapist takes on the characteristics that the client ascribes to the other person if the role play is to have any verisimilitude (e.g. if the client says that a work colleague is rude and abrupt then the therapist should not play this person as polite and considerate as this will undermine the role play). In the following example, the therapist plays the role of the client's friend who is always critical of him and orders him around. The client wants to know why he puts up with such behaviour from his supposed friend.

Therapist: [in role] You were supposed to pick me up at seven. Why the hell were you late?

Client: Sorry. I had trouble with the car.

Therapist: Don't let it happen again. I'm off to a party tonight. I suppose you want to come.

Client: Yes, I would like to come.

Therapist: You can drive me there and home again unless I get lucky with a couple of birds, then you can get lost.

Client: [becoming visibly tense] Okay. I wouldn't want to get in the way.

Therapist: [coming out of role] Is there something you want to say to him but you're holding back?

Client: I want to tell the arrogant bastard to get stuffed!

Therapist: What stops you?

Client: He'll kick me out of the group.

Therapist: And if you were kicked out ...?

Client: [quietly] I'd have no one to talk to or hang around with. I'd be lonely, a real sad case [NATs].

Therapist: Is that why you put up with his behaviour to avoid that outcome? [client nods]

42

ANALYZING A SPECIFIC SITUATION

When a client talks about her problems in general terms it can be difficult for the therapist to tease out her NATs because concrete examples of the problems remain elusive. Also, emotions are more intensely felt in specific situations (e.g. 'I felt scared when it looked as if I was going to be late for the staff meeting') than they are at a general level (e.g. 'I'm concerned about my poor timekeeping'). For these reasons it is important for the therapist to anchor the general problem in a specific context:

Client: There's no specific situation. I'm just a worrier. I always have been. End of story.

Therapist: Are you worried about coming to therapy? [client nods] What thoughts are going through your mind at this very moment to make you feel worried?

Client: What if you can't help me? What if therapy is a waste of time? Therapy might make me worse with you messing around with my mind [NATs].

Instead of seeing worry as amorphous, the therapist isolates and elicits from his client worrying thoughts related to coming to therapy and these provide the entry point to begin to understand her subjective experience. It is important to note that when a client verbalizes her thoughts as questions as in the above dialogue ('What ifs …?'), the therapist needs to help the client to convert these questions into clear statements in order to remove any potential doubt or ambiguity: 'You won't be able to help me – like all the other therapists I've seen. I can't change' and 'Therapy will be a waste of time and I might as well leave now.' Examining NATs is more effective when they are clearly expressed as this allows adaptive responses to be developed to answer them.

43

NATS IN SHORTHAND

This means that NATs can be 'composed of just a few essential words phrased in telegraphic style: "lonely … getting sick … can't stand it … cancer … no good." One word or a short phrase functions as a label for a group of painful memories, fears, or self-reproaches' (McKay *et al.*, 2011: 18). Just as when they are phrased as questions (see previous point and Point 46), NATs phrased in a telegraphic style will be difficult to examine and respond to. In the following exchange, the therapist clarifies the client's shorthand replies:

Therapist: When you didn't get the promotion what thoughts went through your mind to make you feel so angry?

Client: Typical … not again … why? That's what I was thinking.

Therapist: It is important for us to expand those words into sentences so we can get the full meaning behind the words. Okay? [client nods] Can you make it clear what you mean by 'typical'?

Client: Well, typical is typical. I don't know what else to say.

Therapist: Okay. Does it mean, for example, that your company was acting in its typical way of fairness and loyalty when you didn't get the promotion?

(The therapist is giving the opposite meaning to what he hypothesizes will be the client's actual reply; see last paragraph of Point 35.)

Client: Not likely! It's typical of the way those bastards do business: it's who you know, not what you've achieved, that gets you promoted. [first NAT]

Therapist: What does 'not again' mean?

Client: This is the second time I haven't got the promotion.

Therapist: And if that's true, what does that mean to you?

Client: There's a conspiracy against me in the company because I don't toe the line. [second NAT]

Therapist: And can you expand on your third thought 'why me'?

Client: They've got it in for me because I speak my mind and I'm definitely not a brown-noser like some of my colleagues. [third NAT]

Therapist: Have we now got all the meanings behind those shorthand expressions?

Client: I think that's about it. If anything else comes to mind, I'll let you know. We've changed short-hand into longhand, so to speak.

SYMPTOM INDUCTION

In Point 40 we looked at encouraging clients to expose themselves to feared situations they usually avoid in order to reveal their hot thoughts. Wells explains that 'another type of exposure task depends on exposure to internal bodily cues. The elicitation of bodily sensations or cognitive symptoms that are the focus of preoccupation and/or misinterpretation can provide access to a wide range of cognitions concerning danger' (1997: 67). In panic disorder, clients fear arousing certain bodily sensations such as breathlessness, palpitations or dizziness as these signal an imminent disaster involving, respectively, suffocation, heart attack or fainting (see Point 31). Catastrophic cognitions can be elicited by encouraging clients to engage in interoceptive exposure exercises (i.e. inducing feared bodily sensations) like running on the spot, spinning in a chair, holding one's breath, shaking one's head from side to side or hyperventilating (Clark and Beck, 2012). For example, a client who breathed through a narrow straw for two minutes became breathless, felt he was being smothered and would suffocate unless he took deep breaths and/or went outside to get some fresh air in order to save himself.

Health anxiety is 'a condition that consists of either a preoccupation with having a serious illness or a fear of developing a serious illness, despite medical reassurance that this is not an issue' (Willson and Veale, 2009: 3). One of the maintaining factors in health anxiety is the person spending too much time focused on her bodily sensations or changes (attentional fixation). Selective attention experiments teach the client that focusing on normal, but usually unnoticed, bodily sensations (e.g. tingling, twinges, aches) increases her awareness of these sensations and their intensity; subsequent preoccupation with these sensations leads to the worrying conclusion that something could be seriously wrong with her such as 'This tingling means I'm getting multiple sclerosis' (hot thought) and another trip to the doctor is undertaken. When her attention is focused externally, the client is far less likely to notice her bodily sensations.

45

BEHAVIOURAL ASSIGNMENTS

These can be used with any problem where it is difficult to elicit the client's NATs. For example, a client said he would feel inexplicably sad if he cleared out the spare room of his old possessions, but 'I desperately need the room for a guest bedroom'. He agreed to start the task that weekend and record his thoughts on a Daily Thought Record (DTR) form (see Point 47). At the next session, he said that clearing out his 'old stuff' triggered pleasant memories of his younger days which he contrasted with the present: 'The happiest part of my life is behind me. Everything is dull and grey now. Where did my life go?' (NATs). Another client was procrastinating over writing an article for an academic journal but said he was baffled by his continuing delay in 'getting down to it'. He said that he would start that evening and record his accompanying thoughts. At the next session, his DTR form revealed how he had made himself very angry by imagining his finished article being rejected or subjected to extensive revision: 'How dare they treat my work like this. Who are they to criticize me? They should automatically accept it after all my hard work. I'm not going to let those bastards pull me down to their level by tearing my article apart!' (hot thoughts).

Sometimes the behavioural assignment can be carried out in the session in order to uncover the client's NATs. A client agreed to start filling out her 'boring' tax self-assessment form but quickly became frustrated with the task, screwed up the form and threw it to the floor: 'It's so boring. I can't make head or tail of it. The damn form makes me feel I'm stupid' [hot thoughts]. Another client who avoided cold-calling local businesses, even though it was a key way of selling himself to them as a stress management trainer, agreed to make a cold-call from the therapist's office. The call lasted a couple of minutes and the client put down the phone with a deep sigh and said 'they weren't interested'. When the therapist asked him what that meant to him, he said: 'I feel they are rejecting me, not just what I have to offer. Each rejection will ultimately destroy my confidence' [NATs]. Cold calling had become a hot (emotionally charged) issue.

ELICITING KEY NATS FROM LESS IMPORTANT COGNITIVE DATA

As David M. Clark has observed, not all automatic thoughts are clinically useful: 'Anyone who is at all distressed will have an enormous number of negative thoughts, most of which are totally irrelevant. They're sort of rubbish, really. They're not driving the system' (quoted in Weishaar, 1993: 112). Therefore, the therapist needs to sift through this cognitive outpouring carefully in order to pinpoint the hot thoughts that are 'doing the emotional damage'. For example, a client may provide reflections on his thinking in a particular situation rather than the actual thoughts – as this client does when he muses on a boardroom incident: 'Hmm. I think I was possibly anxious because I was wondering what the chairman thought of me when I didn't have the exact figures he wanted. It was something along those lines.' In order to uncover the actual thoughts, the therapist, through imagery, helps the client to recreate the boardroom incident in the present: 'Oh God! I've shown myself up as a complete incompetent. The chairman has lost all faith in me. That's the end of my career with this company.'

Clients can often readily report streams of thoughts connected to their difficulties but omit key disturbance-inducing NATs. In the following example, the client says she feels 'terribly guilty' about her daughter's behaviour, but guilt-inducing thoughts are not evident in the way she talks about the problem:

Client: I do feel terribly guilty about what my daughter is getting up to. You know, things like staying out late, bunking off school, mixing with bad company, won't do what I tell her to. I think to myself, 'Is she on drugs? What's going to happen to her if she keeps on like this?' These things are always on my mind. Maybe I should have it out with her once and for all. She's driving me around the bend.

Running parallel with this first stream of thoughts is a second one containing the client's appraisals of herself or the situation. The therapist helps the client to 'tune into' this second stream in order to locate her distressing thoughts:

Therapist: You said you felt terribly guilty about your daughter's behaviour. What thoughts make you feel so guilty?

Client: I didn't bring her up right. It's my fault that she behaves as she does. If I'd been a good mother she wouldn't have turned out like this. I'm a bad mother. [NATs, underlying assumption: 'If I'd been a good mother she wouldn't have turned out like this', and a core belief – 'I'm a bad mother'. Categorizing her cognitions in this way needs to be discussed with and confirmed by the client. Asking for NATs does not mean that is all the therapist will get!]

Beck (2011) says that clients often report interpretations of their thoughts instead of the actual thoughts. For example, in response to the therapist's question of what goes through the client's mind each time she volunteers to work late, she replies: 'I'm overcompensating for previous career uncertainties' (interpretation). The client's 'previous career uncertainties' were a succession of 'going nowhere jobs. Now I know where I'm going I need to make up for lost time.' Armed with this information, the therapist asks: 'What thoughts drive you to make up for lost time?' The client replies: 'I've got to prove to my boss and work colleagues that I'm as good and competent as they are.'

When clients are asked the 'What was going through your mind?' type of question, they frequently reply with rhetorical questions such as 'How could I have done that?', 'What's the use in trying?' or 'Why does this always happen to me?' Rhetorical questions are not seeking an answer as the speaker implies that the answer is obvious enough; such questions are filled with emotional thoughts. Each client is encouraged by the therapist to answer their own question in order to make explicit what is implied: respectively, 'I did do that bad thing because I'm wicked' (guilt); 'There's no point in trying. Nothing ever goes right for me' (depression); and 'This always happens to me. It's the story of my life. It's not fair' (hurt).

SEPARATING SITUATIONS, THOUGHTS AND FEELINGS

CBT states that it is our interpretations of events rather than the events themselves that produce our emotional reactions; therefore it is important that clients make this connection if they are to profit from CBT. When clients discuss their problems it is often in a jumbled manner (understandably so) with no clear separation between situations, thoughts and feelings, and they often blame the situation itself for how they feel, e.g. 'My husband makes me angry when he goes off to play golf every Sunday morning.' In order to illustrate to clients the mediational role of their thinking in producing their emotional reactions to events they are shown how to use the first three columns of the Daily Thought Record (DTR; see Appendix 2). The DTR is a five-column worksheet that helps 'clients learn to distinguish between situations, thoughts and feelings, identify inaccurate thinking, and develop more balanced appraisals' (Tinch and Friedberg, 1996: 1).

In the early sessions of therapy, clients are taught to focus on the first three columns (situations, thoughts and emotions) in order to gain practice at detecting their negative automatic thoughts (NATs) and recognizing how they are connected to the distressing emotions they experience in specific situations; once clients are able to do this, they can then turn their attention to challenging their NATs. To return to the above example:

Situation	NATs	Emotion
Husband going off to play golf on a Sunday morning	'He should want to be with me but as he doesn't, this means he's stopped loving me. Why the hell is golf more important than me? I'm a golf widow and he doesn't give a damn.'	Angry

Clients are asked to rate the believability of their NATs and the intensity of their emotions using a 0–100 per cent scale. The client rated the believability of her NATs at 80 per cent and the intensity of her anger at 85 per cent. These ratings are important in order to determine collaboratively the cut-off point for investigation of the scores, e.g. thoughts and feelings below 50 per cent are not explored. However, if some clients get bored with providing ratings as it can become mechanical, then the therapist should drop the procedure (clients often know which are the key thoughts and intense feelings to focus on without the ratings).

DTRs should not be given to the client if she does not agree with the cognitive model (e.g. 'My husband makes me angry. That's the whole problem') or is unwilling to fill out the forms (e.g. 'I came here for help, not bloody form-filling!'). Until such difficulties are dealt with, filling out the DTRs will have to wait. For example, the client did eventually see and accept the thought–feeling link by the therapist asking her how she would feel if her husband: (1) stayed at home with her on a Sunday morning and made a fuss of her ('Happy because he wants to be with me'); (2) stayed at home and read the newspaper ('Hurt because I don't deserve to be ignored'); (3) stayed at home but felt morose ('Guilty because I've stopped him doing what he really enjoys'); and (4) stayed at home but only went through the motions of being pleasant to her ('Anxious because he resents me and therefore he might find someone else'). Filling out the DTR forms helped the client to take ownership of her thoughts and feelings rather than blaming her husband's behaviour for them. Beck *et al.* (1985) suggest encouraging clients to put their 'he/she/it makes me feel' statements into the active voice ('I make myself angry') rather than the passive voice ('My husband makes me angry').

Obviously it takes time and effort for clients to learn the differences between situations, thoughts and emotions, and mistakes frequently occur. For example, a client puts 'I feel anxious that I might not get the job' in the NATs column when, in fact, 'anxious' should go in the emotion column and 'I might not get the job' in the situation column (this is a realistic view of his job interview). In order to discover what his NATs are, the client needs to ask himself what it means to him if he does not get the job: 'No decent employer will ever want me. I'll never get a good job, only menial work.'

48

DISTINGUISHING BETWEEN THOUGHTS AND FEELINGS

Inserting the word 'feel' into a sentence does not turn the sentence into a feeling. People frequently say 'I feel' when they actually mean 'I think', such as 'I feel that my son and me are slowly drifting apart' (watching soap operas, for example, shows how dominant are 'I feel' statements over 'I think' statements). People would probably be annoyed if they were frequently corrected when they misused 'I feel' statements: 'When you say "I feel that my son and me are slowly drifting apart" what you really mean is "I think that my son and me are slowly drifting apart".' However, in CBT it is crucial to make such corrections (but not incessantly or condescendingly) because by modifying dysfunctional thoughts distressing feelings are moderated; so clients need to learn to distinguish between genuine thoughts and emotions. Also, if this distinction is not made, clients will believe that their 'feelings' are being challenged when it is their thoughts that are actually being targeted for examination:

> Feelings are not open to dispute; they are phenomenological [subjective] experiences for which only the individual has data. You cannot argue with such subjective states, whereas thoughts, beliefs, and opinions are open to challenge.
>
> (Walen *et al.*, 1992: 98)

Greenberger and Padesky suggest as a general rule that 'moods [e.g. anxiety, depression, guilt, shame, anger] can be identified in one descriptive word. If it takes you more than one word to describe a mood, you may be describing a thought' (1995: 28). For example, a client might say 'I feel like I'll never be able to overcome this problem', which might be converted by the therapist into 'You have this thought that you will never be able to overcome this problem. How do you feel with that thought in mind?' The client might reply with another 'feel' statement: 'I feel that therapy won't be able to help me.' The therapist can point out that the client has now given her two thoughts and then ask again how he would feel with those thoughts in mind: 'Depressed.' It is important that clients express their thoughts in the first person singular, such as 'I'll always be a failure' or 'No one likes me', in order to claim authorship of these thoughts rather than distance themselves from them by using an impersonal voice: 'One would see oneself as a failure in those circumstances' or 'Everyone thinks at some time in their life that no one likes them' (Neenan and Dryden, 2000).

Some clients may use one word to describe their feelings such as 'bad', 'crap' or 'shit'. Unfortunately, these kinds of one-word descriptions, though vivid, do not pinpoint which one-word emotions cognitive behaviour therapists are looking for. By asking the client about his thoughts (e.g. 'I let down my best friend when he needed me. He's always there for me. I behaved very badly') and behaviour (e.g. 'I keep on trying to make it up to him in all sorts of ways'), the therapist is able to reveal the client's 'shit' feeling as guilt – the client violated his moral code of how he should behave towards his best friend ('I should always be there for him like he is for me and I wasn't there when he was in serious trouble'). The client can then decide to use the term 'guilt' or stay with his own idiosyncratic usage.

49

ANSWERING BACK

Once clients have elicited their negative automatic thoughts (NATs) and understood the differences between situations, thoughts and feelings, they are now ready to examine their NATs in various ways in order to develop more helpful and adaptive responses to them (see Points 50–62). Beck *et al.* state that 'the therapist's major task is to help the patient think of reasonable responses to his negative cognitions … to differentiate between a realistic accounting of events and an accounting distorted by idiosyncratic meanings' (1979: 164).

In helping a client to develop these 'reasonable responses', the therapist should allow him sufficient time to think things through as this might be his first attempt to formulate a constructive reply to his negative cognitions. The philosopher John Campbell describes philosophy as 'thinking in slow motion' in order to consider carefully some of the ideas we may have adopted far too quickly and seem to be stuck with. Slowing down our thinking allows us to see both the 'mental moves' we have made in order to subscribe to these ideas and the alternative perspectives that are available to us. We believe that both therapists and clients, if interested, can find a rich source of ideas in philosophy to help them widen and deepen their discussions about coping adaptively with life's vicissitudes. Two such texts are William Irvine's *A Guide to the Good Life* (2009) and *A Slap in the Face* (2013).

As we have seen in the section on detecting NATs, idiosyncratic meaning (e.g. 'My life is over') can make dealing with an objectively unpleasant situation (e.g. losing one's job after 20 years with the same company) much more difficult (e.g. the client says he feels 'overwhelmed with sadness and despair'). Encouraging clients to look at the situation in more realistic ways reduces the intensity of their distressing feelings (e.g. 'My life with that company is over and I still feel upset about it, but not to the same extent as I did. I now realize that my life still has new possibilities and opportunities if I want to seek them out').

In order to achieve this outcome, clients are taught to regard their NATs as hypotheses about themselves, others and the world so that they can be subjected to reason and reality-testing (see Point 11). If a particular automatic thought proves accurate rather than distorted (e.g. 'I have no friends at the present time'), then ways to tackle this situation would be explored such as the client learning to enquire about other people's lives and interests instead of always wanting to be the centre of attention which then pushes people away.

Examining clients' NATs is not based on the therapist trying to prove to her client that his thinking is wrong while hers is right or the therapist adopting the role of a prosecutor in a courtroom and trying to 'catch out' the client when discussing his thoughts (e.g. 'You say you're all alone in the world but you told me earlier that neighbours pop in to see how you are and you get phone calls from your family. It's not true then, is it?'). Examination involves collaborative investigation to develop adaptive responses to the client's NATs.

Some therapists, particularly those new to CBT, might believe (incorrectly) that as soon as they hear the possibility of a cognitive distortion in clients' accounts of their problems they have to challenge it immediately rather than letting their clients have their say:

> The unfortunate effect [of this overzealousness] is that of micromanaging the clients' thinking, and this can cause a strain in the therapeutic relationship. By contrast, competent CBT clinicians take note of some of the key comments their clients are making, respond empathically, and then wait for a natural pause in the discussion to summarize the sorts of negative cognitive content that the clients are revealing.
>
> (Newman, 2013: 154)

50

WEIGHING THE EVIDENCE

Weighing the evidence for and against a particular automatic thought 'is probably the most common method of cognitive restructuring [thought and belief change]' (Moorey, 1990: 240). For example, a client says that 'nothing ever goes right for me' and lists past and present setbacks and failures to support this thought, and cannot think of any contradictory evidence; in his mind, this 'proves my case':

Therapist: You said you've moved house recently. How did that go?

Client: It was all right.

Therapist: So did the house move go right for you?

Client: Yes, I suppose so.

Therapist: How long have you been married?

Client: Fourteen years.

Therapist: How would you describe those fourteen years?

Client: They've been happy most of the time. Okay, so you've found two things that have gone right for me and maybe there are other things I can't see at the present time. Am I supposed to suddenly become a positive thinker then?

Therapist: Positive thinking doesn't usually consider evidence but realistic thinking does. I want you to try and stand back from your thought, 'nothing ever goes right for me', and consider all the evidence, not just part of it (the therapist helps the client to uncover further evidence against the thought). How might you respond now to that thought?

Client: Well, I suppose it would be more accurate to say that 'Sometimes things go right for me and sometimes they don't and, therefore, it's important for me to keep things in perspective.' I'd feel a bit better if I can remember that. Looking for evidence is a strain on the brain!

Difficulties can arise over what constitutes evidence: typically, the therapist is seeking facts to support, modify or disconfirm her client's thoughts while he is furnishing information based on 'gut feelings' or assumptions. Newman (1989) suggests which information can qualify as objective evidence and which cannot:

1   Confirmational data – the client obtains 'the hard facts' (objective, direct and unambiguous) such as 'My wife has told me she's having an affair'.
2   Observational data – what the client has noticed which may point to a hard fact but the client could be making incorrect inferences like 'I saw my wife laughing while she was talking to a man in the high street and she was standing very close to him, so she must be having an affair with him'.
3   Conjectural data – stems from the client's hunches, impressions, feelings, intuition, 'I just know my wife is having an affair. You know what you know, do you know what I mean?'

Newman (1989) states that the level of evidence therapists ideally strive for is confirmational data. However, some clients will settle for observational or conjectural data but the therapist needs to stress the limitations of such data and the potential problems of employing it such as the client accusing his wife of having an affair, based on his insecurities (conjectural data), which then triggers a crisis in the relationship.

The need to weigh and test evidence in CBT rests on the assumption that if our thinking is more accurately aligned with events in the external world (independent of our perception of it), we will then experience better mental health because we are less likely to engage in distorted thinking and experience the associated emotional upsets. Dobson and Dobson (2009) call this perspective 'the realist assumption'. CBT also explores clients' inner experiences – how they reach their views about themselves and the world, the meanings they attach to events. Therefore, the cognitive behavioural therapist is constantly moving between the external and internal worlds of the client and trying to uncover the private meaning about a public event (e.g. moving house) which is causing her so much distress.

51

CONSTRUCTING ALTERNATIVE EXPLANATIONS

This technique shows clients that there is more than one way of looking at any given situation. Blackburn and Davidson suggest:

> Asking the patient to list alternative interpretations of a situation and then *establishing the realistic probability* of each interpretation is a powerful technique, as it does not reject the original negative interpretation, unlikely as it might be, and contrasts it with more likely interpretations.
>
> (1995: 76; emphasis in original)

In the following example, the client believes that the workshop she ran was a 'flop' because two evaluation forms out of 20 were critical:

Therapist:	Okay, that's one view of the situation. What about the eighteen evaluation forms that were favourable?
Client:	Well, I suppose it was reasonably successful then.
Therapist:	Any other ways of looking at the situation?
Client:	They felt sorry for me and that's why they gave me favourable feedback.
Therapist:	How likely is it that they felt sorry for you?
Client:	Highly unlikely. They were not a touchy-feely lot. They seemed quite hard to please in some ways.
Therapist:	Any other explanations for getting favourable feedback?
Client:	It was a fluke, a one off.

Therapist: It's hard to tell at this stage as it was your first workshop. Are you planning to do more? [client nods]. Could there be other interpretations rather than it was a fluke?

Client: I gave a good performance.

Therapist: Anything else?

Client: They didn't have to pay to attend the workshop, so they scored me higher on the evaluation forms than they would have done if they were paying.

Therapist: Do you think they would put up with low standards just because they weren't paying? You did say they 'seemed quite hard to please in some ways'.

Client: I very much doubt they would have done that. I wouldn't if I was in the group.

Therapist: [writing on a whiteboard] So to sum up: your original thought about the workshop was that it was a 'flop' because two evaluation forms were critical. However, eighteen forms were favourable and based on this fact other explanations were: the workshop was reasonably successful, people felt sorry for you, it was a fluke, you gave a good performance and people didn't have to pay. Which explanation seems the most probable in the light of our discussion?

The client chose 'a good performance and I suppose that's why it was reasonably successful'; however, she still wondered if there were some 'fluky elements' involved in the success of the workshop and therefore the therapist suggested she run several more workshops over the next several months in order to collect data on her performance to resolve this issue: 'Do I have real skill or was the success of that first workshop sheer luck?'

52

IDENTIFYING COGNITIVE DISTORTIONS

In Point 2 we listed some common cognitive distortions or biases such as mind-reading, labelling and jumping to conclusions that are the results of faulty information processing when a person is emotionally upset (for a fuller list of cognitive distortions see Leahy *et al.*, 2012). Westbrook *et al.* (2011: 172) point out that these distortions 'reflect normal fluctuations in our information-processing styles, and they only become a problem when the bias is chronic or too extreme'. The client can be given a list of cognitive distortions and asked by the therapist if he can identify the ones that are usually found in his thinking.

For example, a client with social anxiety said: 'I know that when I walk into a room people are thinking "he's boring, so I'll keep away from him" or if they do start talking to me then they quickly move away because they're thinking "he's so uninteresting".' The client quickly identified mind-reading as one of his key cognitive distortions, but then added, 'I do believe I can read minds, it's true'. The therapist conducted an immediate experiment to test the client's ability to mind-read by writing the words 'Mickey Mouse' on a piece of paper; the client was unable to say what had been written down.

Mind-reading can be seen as a form of projection: 'The thoughts patients believe others are having about them are usually the very thoughts they are having about themselves' (Persons, 1989: 113). In the above example, if the client thinks he is boring, he is likely to conclude that others think in a similar way about him. The important point is for the client to read his own mind in a non-distorted way and stop attempting to read the minds of others (Neenan and Dryden, 2002). These discussions (and experiment) with the therapist convinced the client that he was not a mind-reader: 'Realistically, I don't know what people think of me. I can ask them or go and talk to them to get some idea. Even if some people do find me boring that doesn't prove that I am, just that I can't interest everyone.'

Another key distortion of the client's was all or nothing thinking: 'People are either boring like me or very interesting and fascinating to talk to as most people are.' As McKay *et al.* point out: 'Since your interpretations are extreme, your emotional reactions are extreme' (2011: 29). The client found it hard to see the middle ground between these two extreme positions: that people can be seen as both boring and interesting, e.g. 'She's really interesting when she talks about her work as a doctor, but when she starts talking about opera – her great passion – I feel like dropping off to sleep.' Once the client had learnt to direct more of his attention to the external environment and away from his excessive self-focus on his assumed inadequacies, he found over time that he could be reasonably interesting to some people some of the time and not everyone he met held him transfixed with their supposedly fascinating conversation.

53

LOOKING AT THE ADVANTAGES AND DISADVANTAGES

This technique helps clients to tease out the advantages and disadvantages of adhering to a particular thought (e.g. 'Being on my own keeps me safe') or engaging in a specific behaviour (e.g. procrastination). Through discussion of each advantage and disadvantage, clients can learn to revise their self-defeating thoughts and change their counterproductive behaviours. Wells states that 'an effort should be made to generate more disadvantages than advantages ... when the disadvantages of maintaining a behaviour or attitude outweigh the advantages, the individual should be more motivated to change' (1997: 72). The advantages and disadvantages of the above thought were written on the therapist's whiteboard:

'BEING ON MY OWN KEEPS ME SAFE'

Advantages	Disadvantages
1 'I won't get rejected any more and feel terrible'	1 'And I won't have any more relationships to feel terrible about'
2 'I won't have anyone bossing me around'	2 'And I'll miss out on opportunities to learn to be more assertive in relationships'
3 'I can control my own life'	3 'And what an empty one it will be to control'

4 'I won't have to worry about becoming jealous and my emotions running riot'	4 'All I have to worry about is becoming an emotional desert'
	5 'My life is mapped out for me in all its bleak solitude'
	6 'Life without a relationship is not much of a life. I don't want that'

At the end of this exercise the thought had no further appeal to the client, but she wanted to learn to be more resilient in coping with the vicissitudes of relationships ('I can also be safe in a relationship if I learn to take the rough with the smooth and not see the end of a relationship as a great catastrophe'). For example, the client felt terrible when she was rejected because she suffered a double rejection: from her boyfriend, then herself ('I can't be any good if he's left me'). Part of developing a resilient outlook was for her to deal with the first rejection without creating a second, self-inflicted one ('He's rejected me but I'm not going to reject myself because of it'); understand that 'rejection' is a loaded term (i.e. charged with underlying self-denigratory meanings such as worthlessness); and realize that relationships often follow a natural history (i.e. they eventually stop functioning happily or productively) and therefore it is time for her to move on instead of seeing relationships as inevitably ending in rejection, despair and loneliness.

If some clients find the advantages/disadvantages technique unproductive, Hanna (2002) suggests intentions and counterintentions (these are not viewed negatively) as they reflect conflicting values and goals in a person's life. For example, a client pulled out of buying a house with his partner at the last moment because of his doubts about the endurability of their relationship. He said his intention was to be happy in a 'totally fulfilling relationship'; his counterintention to this goal was to remain single 'and play the field as I might eventually find the ideal woman'. The intention and counterintention were discussed in detail and then re-evaluated. It emerged that 'playing the field to find the ideal woman' was just a typical male fantasy and he admitted that the reality would be 'spending my evenings alone watching lots of crap television'. He opted for the intention but realized that insisting on a 'totally fulfilling relationship' meant the eradication of all doubt from his mind – doubts demonstrated that the relationship would surely fail. He now accepted that any major life decision is usually accompanied by doubts rather than made with complete confidence and certainty. He was reconciled with his partner and they bought a house together.

54

DEFINING TERMS

This process concentrates clients' minds on the imprecision of their language in describing themselves or their problems. For example, a client whose manuscript was rejected by a publisher stated: 'Because they didn't want it, this makes me a failure.'

Therapist: When you say you're a failure because the publisher rejected your manuscript, do you mean a failure as an author, man, person?

Client: As an author.

Therapist: How does rejection by a particular publisher make you a failure as an author?

Client: Well, it feels like it.

Therapist: Well, as we've discussed previously, feelings are not facts or a higher form of truth. If you are genuinely a failure as an author then you had better not waste any more time on a hopeless cause. Now, when will all the evidence be in about whether you're a failure as an author?

Client: Some years from now. I shouldn't decide on the basis of one rejection.

Therapist: So what would be an accurate description of your current situation?

Client: I've failed to impress one publisher with my manuscript but that doesn't mean I'm a failure as an author.

Therapist: What does it mean then?

Client: That I'm a struggling author who needs to keep on struggling if I hope to make my mark in the literary world. It's going to be some struggle though.

Some clients might complain that defining terms is just semantic games (e.g. 'Change the words around and then I'll feel better, is that it?') but, in fact, it has a very serious purpose. Using words like 'failure', 'useless', 'worthless' or 'no good' to define oneself are not only dangerous overgeneralizations – a person might become depressed and consider suicide through such self-labelling – but are hopelessly inadequate and inaccurate in capturing the complexity and uniqueness of the self. Semantic precision helps clients to be clear and accurate about events (e.g. 'I've failed my driving test twice') and what can be done about them (e.g. 'I shall try for a third time') instead of focusing on what they believe they are (e.g. 'I'm totally useless. I might as well give up now') which will prevent them learning from their mistakes and restricting their self-development such as not persevering in the face of setbacks. The therapist needs to keep clients on their toes by asking them to define their terms instead of letting them assume the meaning of the terms is mutually understood and agreed.

However, it is important that therapists do not become 'meaning maniacs', i.e. asking their clients what they mean by the terms that they use and then asking for the meaning of the new terms that the clients use to explain the old terms ... and so on as this will develop into an infinite regress of meaning about meaning. This process will exhaust both therapist and client without reaching any helpful conclusions about which terms are meaningful in discussing problems (e.g. rating only the specific behaviour or action) and which are meaningless (e.g. rating the self; see Point 93). Defining terms is not an end in itself: it is a means of establishing semantic clarity so that a more informed discussion of these terms can be undertaken.

55

REATTRIBUTION

Reattribution helps clients to step back from and look at the many contributions to an adverse outcome. Thus, a client who blames herself for causing a bad outcome can be helped to see that she cannot be responsible for all the factors that led to this outcome. Self-blame for 'causing' negative outcomes is particularly evident in guilt and depression (Dattilio and Freeman, 1992). For example, a client said that she felt guilty because her 30-year-old son was 'not fulfilling his potential, just drifting through life and drinking heavily', and blamed herself for her son's difficulties ('I've failed him somewhere along the line. It's my fault he's like that'). This statement reflected the client's assumption of omnipotence, i.e. she has the power to control her son's destiny.

By listing as many factors as possible that have contributed to her son's difficulties (e.g. never keeping a job for long, being in debt, falling behind in his maintenance payments to his ex-wife, heavy drinking, falling out with his neighbours, not caring about his appearance), the client realized eventually that her ability to influence, let alone control, her son's life was severely limited ('He doesn't pay any attention to me. He just accuses me of nagging him all the time which he gets angry about. At the end of the day, it's his life and he's responsible for it. I hope things improve for him'). Reattribution is not meant to let clients 'off the hook' but to help them assess accurately their level of responsibility in producing a particular outcome. In the above example, the client said, 'I'm probably not helping him with my nagging, so I've told him I'll be there for him whenever he asks for my help but I'm not going to pester him any more.' Each factor contributing to the outcome can be given a percentage rating – the total score must not go beyond 100 per cent – and the client's initial rating of responsibility (90 per cent) can be recalculated (20 per cent) on the basis of all the factors she has overlooked in contributing to her son's predicament.

56

DECATASTROPHIZING

This is taking the 'horror' (emotional disturbance) out of a feared event by encouraging clients to see themselves dealing adaptively with their catastrophic predictions. Catastrophic thinking is often generated by 'What if …?' statements such as 'What if I panic in the supermarket?' or 'What if I fail my exams?'(see Point 39). Barlow and Cerny state that 'the general strategy for decatastrophizing is to encourage the client to outline specifically the consequences of the feared event' (1988: 132). For each catastrophic consequence, the client can be helped to generate problem-solving alternatives:

'WHAT IF I PANIC IN THE SUPERMARKET?'

Consequences	Alternatives
'I'll make a complete fool of myself. People will laugh at me and think I'm pathetic.'	'I could be a coper instead of a fool and surprise myself. What people think and do I have no control over, but I don't have to think I'm pathetic or laugh at myself. Having panic attacks is not a crime.'
'I'll never be able to go into that supermarket again as people will remember me and point me out.'	'The only person who is going to remember is me. I'm assuming that my panic attack is burned into people's memories. That's nonsense. People will only point me out if I walk around the supermarket naked!'

Beck *et al.* observe that 'when predicting dire consequences, the anxious patient does not utilize all of the information available to him and rarely takes into account his past dire predictions that failed to materialize' (1985: 208). This information includes rescue factors in the situation such as staff and maybe some customers coming to the client's aid if she does have a panic attack in the supermarket; any embarrassment or humiliation she experiences will be time-limited, not suffered indefinitely; high levels of anxiety are bearable rather than unbearable and she has coped successfully with her panic attacks in other situations. Barlow and Craske (1989) propose that decatastrophizing can be summed up as 'So what?', i.e. the client can learn to accept and tolerate what she fears. However, these authors concede that the 'so what' strategy would be inappropriate with client fears of death or loss of significant others; focusing on overestimation of danger is the more appropriate strategy in these cases, e.g. a client who fears dying in a plane crash, dwells on a recent reported crash thereby increasing the likelihood in his mind that it will happen to his flight tomorrow, but is unwilling to consider 'the base rate – that is, that air travel is considerably safer than any other means of traveling the same distance' (Leahy, 2003: 161) though the risk of the plane crashing cannot be reduced to zero.

Edelman (2006) advances two important things to keep in mind while developing a balanced appraisal of our fears:

1 Over 90 per cent of the things we fear never happen (keeping a record of catastrophic predictions and comparing these with what actually happened would bear this out).
2 The consequences of your fears coming true are rarely catastrophic but, instead, usually manageable. However, if a perceived catastrophe does occur such as having your house repossessed and being made homeless, then the struggle to adapt to this grim reality while gruelling may also reveal eventually that you are stronger than you ever thought you could be in such circumstances (Neenan, 2009).

Newman suggests a creative challenge to negative 'What if …?' thinking by asking clients to give equal consideration to positive 'What if …?' thinking:

Clients rarely if ever give equal time to the positive, literally *opposite* question, 'What if I succeed?' Therein lies a fundamental cognitive bias, because an objective assessment of future outcomes requires the careful consideration of both the positive and negative possibilities.

(2000: 140; emphasis in original)

57

EXPLORING DOUBLE STANDARDS

Some clients apply a standard much more strictly to themselves than they do to others. For example, a mother condemned herself as bad when her child fell over and injured himself while out playing ('I can't be any good as a mother for letting this happen'), but has words of sympathy and understanding, not condemnation, for a friend whose child suffered a similar misfortune ('It can't be helped that children injure themselves when they're out playing. You can't keep them cooped up indoors all day, can you? You musn't blame yourself for what happened'). By eliciting the client's reasoning for this difference in her approach towards herself and her friend, the therapist can understand the basis for the client's double standards ('I have to be the perfect mother for my son to make up for not holding the marriage together. I just feel I've always got to be there for him, to protect him from harm, keep him safe'). The client can also be asked to imagine the effect on her friend if she did condemn her: 'She'd feel much worse.'

The therapist can encourage his client to talk to herself in the same sympathetic way she would do to her neighbour in order to answer her NATs: 'It takes two, not one, to hold a marriage together. There is no such thing as a perfect mother, only a mother trying to do her best for her children. It's unrealistic to think I can always keep my son safe from harm. So as a mother, I'm good enough.' Through such self-discussion, double standards can be ditched and replaced with a single standard that is helpful, compassionate and realistic (Burns, 1989). A particularly powerful way of exploring double standards is asking clients if they would teach what they think to their children – 'You're worthless without a partner'. The reply almost always is 'No' as they can see the damaging effects this belief would have on them; so, if they would not teach it to their children, do they want to continue to teach it to themselves? If a client replies 'Yes', then elicit the reasons for teaching this belief and the likely consequences for their children if they internalize it, such as eventually ending up in therapy like the parent.

58

MODIFYING FEARFUL IMAGERY

NATs come in visual as well as verbal form. Some clients find it easier to work with images rather than thoughts to achieve cognitive modification of their NATs. When clients imagine negative events, they often stop at the moment when their worst fear is being realized, as if the 'film' has broken down and they do not see what happens next. For example, a client had graphic images of seeing himself turn into a 'sweating, gibbering, nervous wreck rooted to the spot' when people laughed at him for spilling water over himself when taking a drink during a presentation. Wells suggests it is 'useful to "finish-out" images and take them beyond the worst point. This procedure reduces the amount of distress accompanying the image and shifts the patient out of danger processing mode' (1997: 76). The client is asked to restart the 'film':

Therapist: What's happening right now?
Client: They're still laughing at me. I'm blushing terribly. I'm tongue-tied and still rooted to the spot. I can't move.
Therapist: What about one minute later?
Client: I'm beginning to move about a bit and am beginning to nod my head and attempt to smile as if I'm in on the joke.
Therapist: Are they still laughing as much?
Client: No. The laughter is beginning to die down along with my blushing. I'm taking some quiet deep breaths to get myself more under control. I'm smiling more now and pointing to myself saying 'clumsy fingers'.
Therapist: What's happening five minutes later?

Client: I'm continuing to give the presentation but I'm still feeling a little shaky and tongue-tied. I'm wondering what they think of me but I'm doing my best to focus on the presentation.

Therapist: And thirty minutes later?

Client: I'm much more in control and feeling better. I prove this to myself by having a drink of water without spilling it. There are a few titters when I pick up the glass but after drinking it without spilling any, I stretch out my hand and say to the group 'much better now'. Then it's time for lunch which I feel much relieved by.

The client's imaginal journey through the worst and beyond demonstrates to him that he will not be stuck in that 'awful' moment for ever. The client practised regularly this imagery exercise and later declared: 'I don't think it would be a big deal any longer if it did happen to me. To be honest I'm getting bored with it. So what if I spill water over myself?' The general thrust of imagery modification in CBT is to help clients change the negative direction of their imagery towards positive and more successful coping scenes (Dattilio and Freeman, 1992).

59

BEHAVIOURAL EXPERIMENTS

Behavioural experiments in CBT serve a cognitive purpose: to test the validity of clients' thoughts and beliefs through action assignments, the next stage after in-session verbal discussion of these cognitions. The evidence gathered from these experiments helps clients to construct new problem-solving perspectives. For example, a client who was very self-conscious about being overweight was unhappy about 'not allowing myself to go swimming'. If she went swimming her prediction was: 'People will stare at me and snigger and I won't be able to stay there' (the client said she wanted to stay in the pool for at least 30 minutes). The client anticipated that her level of anxiety would be 85 per cent in carrying out the experiment, but nevertheless wanted to discover if her fears would be realized. The information collected from the experiment was discussed in the next session:

Therapist: What actually happened in the swimming pool?

Client: There were people there of all shapes and sizes, so that was a relief.

Therapist: Okay, but what about your specific prediction, 'People will stare at me and snigger and I won't be able to stay there.' Did that prove true or false?

Client: False. Obviously people looked at me – I was looking around too – but as far as I could tell no one was staring or sniggering at me. There was lots of shouting, laughing and people enjoying themselves.

Therapist: How long did you stay in the pool for?

Client: About an hour.

Therapist: What about your anxiety level? You said that would be 85 per cent.

Client: That came down to about 40 per cent. After about ten or fifteen minutes I was much less self-conscious and focused on my swimming rather than looking at others to see if they were looking at me.

Therapist: So how would you respond to your prediction?

Client: Obviously people did look at me but as far as I was aware no one sniggered at me and I was able to stay there. However, I do need to go once a week if I'm to feel less self-conscious in my swimming costume and see the trip as enjoyable rather than as an ordeal.

The therapist should not assume that just because a behavioural experiment has proved successful that an adaptive cognitive response has been generated. In evaluating the data from the experiment, the client may have concluded: 'If the pool had been less crowded then I would have stood out more and people would have stared and sniggered at me.' In this case, trips to the pool could be arranged when it was less crowded to test this prediction. Also, coping responses would be developed – not only to deal with any possible sniggering but also to stay in the pool and leave when she decided to rather than prematurely because she found the sniggering unbearable.

It is important not to construct experiments in terms of success or failure but to convey to clients that the outcome of an experiment is of interest whatever happens (Bennett-Levy *et al.*, 2004), e.g. information gleaned from the experiment reveals new aspects of the problem which then helps to refine the case conceptualization or the client wants to capitalize on the 'it went well' outcome to speed her progress through the treatment plan. Experiments can also be based on observation (e.g. watching others cope in situations the client fears) or conducting a survey where the client gathers a range of opinions on an issue he is currently struggling with (e.g. 'Does going to restaurants alone mean that someone is a saddo [friendless and inadequate]?').

Butler *et al.* (2008: 109) state that behavioural experiments engage the whole person in learning, so therapists should not be looking 'just for cognitive change, but change across the system as a whole – cognitive, emotional, physical and behavioral'. In our experience, some clients 'jump straight into' carrying out behavioural experiments (i.e. from the first session onwards) once they understand the rationale for them and look forward to the expected quicker progress they can make as a result.

SOCRATIC QUESTIONING (A METHOD OF GUIDED DISCOVERY)

As well as eliciting NATs (see Point 33), Socratic questioning is also employed to assist clients to 'open up' their maladaptive thinking in order to develop alternative interpretations of problematic situations that better fit the facts. As Beck *et al.* observe:

> Questioning leads patients to generate options and solutions that they have not considered ... [and] this approach puts patients in the "questioning mode" (as opposed to the "automatic impulse" mode) so that they will start to evaluate more objectively their various attitudes and beliefs.
>
> (1993: 29)

Also, through such questioning clients are enabled to provide their own replies to their NATs rather than accept any interpretations that might be offered by the therapist. Padesky (1993b) suggests that Socratic questioning consists of four stages: (1) asking informational questions; (2) listening attentively and reflecting back; (3) summarizing newly acquired information; and (4) asking analytical or synthesizing questions to apply the new information to the client's original problem or thought. These four stages are now demonstrated in the following dialogue:

Client: I'm worried about meeting some new people this weekend.
Therapist: Do you know what you're worried about?

Client:	What they will think of me.
Therapist:	What do you think they'll think of you?
Client:	They'll think I'm a rather boring person and limit the time they spend with me. That's what I'm worried about. I'm not exactly the life and soul of the party type. I'm more of a quiet type. That's not a crime, is it?

(These questions have made the problem understandable to both therapist and client – Stage 1.)

Therapist:	Hmm. In listening to you, it seems that you might think that being 'a quiet type' is a crime. Is that true?
Client:	I suppose it is: it shouldn't be a crime but some people like my boisterous work colleagues might think so. If you're quiet you must be boring. That would be their reasoning.
Therapist:	[ponders] Does it have to be your reasoning as well? Is it others' opinions of you that make you boring or do you see yourself as intrinsically boring because you're quiet?
Client:	I never thought of it like that. I suppose I do agree if others think I'm boring.

(The therapist's reflections have brought information into the client's awareness that was currently outside of it – Stage 2.)

Therapist:	And if you didn't agree with others' opinions of you, but thought about this issue more carefully, then what?
Client:	Well, I am a quiet person who is not to everyone's taste, but I don't see myself as intrinsically boring. I have interests, I read a lot. I'm reasonably happy with my life.
Therapist:	So it seems that you can make up your own mind whether or not you consider yourself to be boring rather than agreeing with others'

> opinions of you. You said you have interests, read a lot and are reasonably happy with your life.

(The therapist summarizes the new information that has been revealed – Stage 3.)

Client: That's all true.
Therapist: So how does this information you have just supplied fit in with your original idea that you would agree with others if they thought you were boring?

(The therapist asks a synthesizing question to bring new information to bear on the client's original idea that he is boring if others consider him to be – Stage 4.)

Client: It doesn't fit in. I decide what I am.
Therapist: How will you remind yourself of that?
Client: By writing it down and going over it every day – 'Some people may think I'm boring but I see myself as an interesting person.'

Modelling Socratic questioning for clients helps them to observe and practise this skill as part of their developing role as a self-therapist.

61

EXAGGERATION AND HUMOUR

> Almost by definition, humor involves a creative and sometimes bizarre shift of perspective that makes a previous idea or statement seem "silly" or "funny" from the new viewpoint.
>
> (Dobson and Dobson, 2009: 137)

Humour by exaggeration takes clients' self-defeating ideas to extreme conclusions in order to show them the inherent absurdity of these ideas and thereby generate more realistic views about the problematic situation. In this example, the client has made some accounting errors at work:

Client: I can't help thinking that something dreadful is going to happen because of my mistakes.

Therapist: [with mock seriousness] The company will close down, hundreds will be unemployed, whole industries will disappear overnight, the country will grind to a halt and a global recession will be unleashed.

Client: [laughing] You're laying it on a bit thick aren't you?

Therapist: You did say 'something dreadful is going to happen' because of your mistakes.

Client: Okay, I get the point. It's not dreadful then as that's going over the top, but my boss will probably haul me over the coals for the mistakes. That is realistic.

The use of exaggeration and humour 'may not be a good idea for the patient who is so extremely fragile and vulnerable that he feels ridiculed or criticized by the therapist's humorous

… remarks' (Persons, 1989: 136). The therapist should use these techniques only after a sound therapeutic relationship has been established with her client and emphasize to him that they are directed at his ideas, not him. Once these techniques have been used, feedback should be elicited from the client to determine their impact upon him. Therapists can also poke fun at their own 'strange' ideas to demonstrate that their clients do not have a monopoly on them.

62

WRITING DOWN ALTERNATIVE RESPONSES TO NATS

We have indicated in Point 47 that the first three columns of the daily thought record (DTR) form are used for recording and distinguishing between situations, thoughts and feelings. The process of examining NATs leads to clients filling in column four with their alternative responses to these thoughts (see Appendix 2). These responses should be based on considering all the available evidence and not on the first unconsidered thoughts that pop into the client's mind – no automatic responses! – otherwise these responses may be unrealistic, overly positive or even more dysfunctional than the thoughts they are answering. To return to the example in Point 47, the client was angry (emotion) about her husband going off to play golf on a Sunday morning (situation). Her NATs were:

NATS	Alternative responses	Outcome
'He should want to be with me but as he doesn't, this means he's stopped loving me.' (80%)	'I'm mind-reading again and jumping to conclusions – the wrong ones. He does want to be with me but not all of the time for heaven's sake!' (95%)	Angry (20%)
'Why the hell is golf more important than me?' (80%)	'Golf is important to him on a Sunday morning but it is not more important than me. He's told me that often enough. I need to be reassured over this	

NATS	Alternative responses	Outcome
	issue which is my problem, not his.' (90%)	
'I'm a golf widow and he doesn't give a damn.' (80%)	'A Sunday morning once a week does not make me a golf widow. If he didn't give a damn about my feelings he'd always be on the golf course or out somewhere else.' (90%)	

The client was asked to rate her belief in her alternative responses to her NATs and then re-rate the intensity of her anger (it was originally 85 per cent) in the light of these responses to determine if they had any positive impact on her mood. The client's comment – 'I need to be reassured over this issue' – may point to an intermediate belief (e.g. 'If he doesn't want to be with me all the time, then this proves he doesn't really want to be with me at all') and/or core belief (e.g. 'I'm unloveable'), which would then require examination and modification later in therapy. Filling out DTR forms helps clients to see that cognitive change leads to emotional change; this reduction in emotional intensity (20 per cent angry) can be quickly reversed if her mind is flooded again with NATs. Emotional change is imperfectly achieved and monitoring is required to detect and deal with upsetting thoughts when they appear. As clients gain more competence and confidence in completing these forms, the process of identifying and responding to NATs quickens thereby allowing clients to carry out this process mentally. The DTR forms can always remain on standby if clients need to 'return to basics' intermittently.

The therapist wants to be sure that cognitive change achieved, for example, through the use of DTRs is accompanied by behavioural change – what I (WD) have called cognition with ignition: 'Patients in therapy are engaging in verbal learning, and it is important to assure that their behavior in the real world matches their verbal behavior in the session' (Walen *et al.*, 1992: 169). Homework or between-session assignments is where verbal learning is put into behavioural practice.

RATIONALE FOR HOMEWORK

The therapy session is usually a poor arena for assessing change because of its removal from the client's everyday experience. Assignments carried out between sessions (homework) allow clients to test and modify their maladaptive thoughts and beliefs in real-life situations. Homework – or whatever term clients choose – allows them to apply the skills of CBT with increasing confidence and competence. Also, without homework tasks clients may become 'emotionally constipated' (waiting to 'tell it all' at the next session) instead of dealing with the 'it' (difficulties) as they arise. As Persons observes:

> Situations that arouse powerful affect [emotion] probably involve the patient's key underlying ideas, and the ability to work on these when they are activated offers a potent opportunity for change that would be missed if all therapeutic work took place during therapy sessions.
>
> (1989: 142)

Clients often say they believe intellectually but not emotionally their adaptive responses to their negative thinking. This division between 'head and gut' thinking hinges on clients' degree of belief or conviction in these responses such as when a client says: 'I know up here [tapping head] that I can be happy without a partner but I don't feel it down here [tapping stomach].' In order to test this 'gut truth', the client agrees not to look for a partner for several months and, instead, focus on activities that will help her to become more self-reliant. This assignment helps the client to strengthen her conviction that she can be happy living on her own (i.e. she believes it intellectually and feels it emotionally) and weaken her conviction that she cannot be happy without a partner. When she does decide to look for a partner it is now out of choice, not desperation or need.

Beck *et al.* state that 'the patient is encouraged to view homework as an *integral, vital component* of treatment. Homework is not just an elective, adjunct procedure' (1979: 272; emphasis in original). Therefore, clients are encouraged from the first session onwards to carry out homework tasks rather than delay the implementation of these tasks until they feel comfortable with the CBT format. Homework tasks are agreed collaboratively, but in the early stages of CBT the therapist usually takes a more active role in setting such tasks.

Homework allows clients to develop as a self-therapist in tackling their problems thereby reducing the chances not only of a full-blown relapse (the re-emergence of the original problem) but also the dangers of becoming dependent on the therapist for answers to their problems. Also, carrying out homework tasks accelerates clients' progress towards goal achievement and thereby reduces the time they need to spend in therapy. Some clients might be interested in knowing that

> Studies of psychotherapy process and outcome have produced evidence demonstrating that cognitive behavioural therapy involving homework assignments produces significantly better outcomes than those from therapy consisting entirely of in-session work. This research has also shown that treatment outcome is significantly enhanced when clients complete their homework assignments.
>
> (Kazantzis *et al.*, 2005: 2)

TYPES OF HOMEWORK ASSIGNMENT

These usually include a mixture of cognitive (including imagery) and behavioural assignments. Cognitive assignments include:

1 *Bibliotherapy*. These are reading assignments which help clients to understand their psychological problems not only in more depth but also to learn the CBT methods used for tackling them. There is a substantial CBT self-help literature. Some examples: anxiety disorders (Shafran *et al.*, 2013), relationship problems (Beck, 1988), sleep problems (Espie, 2006), low self-esteem (Fennell, 1999), depression (Leahy, 2010), learning life coaching skills (Neenan and Dryden, 2014). Self-help literature is usually seen as an adjunct to therapy, not as a substitute for it.

2 *Listening*. Clients can be encouraged to record each session in order for them to reflect upon its content away from the therapist's office; some clients may listen several times to each session to gain maximum therapeutic benefit from it. Clients often process information poorly during sessions because they are emotionally upset or they may be reluctant to admit they do not understand the points the therapist is making. On their own, they are less likely to feel inhibited or distracted and therefore more able to focus on the session. If a client does not want his or her sessions recorded, then the therapist would comply with this request.

3 *Writing*. Filling out Daily Thought Record (DTR) forms or variations of them is a staple homework task. These forms help clients to record and respond to their upsetting

thinking in more objective ways (see Points 47 and 62). Writing assignments can encompass any project that will benefit clients in tackling their problems such as a client who agreed to write an essay entitled, 'Is endless people-pleasing the best way to develop self-acceptance?', and concluded at the end of it that people-pleasing was 'psychological servitude that I'm determined to get free of and focus more on being myself'. An action plan was then developed to translate determination into an achievable reality and find out what 'being myself' actually means.

4   *Coping imagery*. This task helps clients to imagine themselves coping in situations where they fear an unpleasant outcome, e.g. a client who fears that 'I will be dumped after my first date if I'm not witty and good fun all evening' imagines himself carrying on a conversation without straining to be witty and good fun, and keeping an open mind as to how the evening will turn out.

5   *Inaction versus action imagery* (Neenan and Palmer, 1998). Clients who are unmotivated to engage in problem-solving and thereby remain stranded in problem-perpetuating are asked to imagine graphically the consequences of not dealing with their difficulties (e.g. endless procrastination, never going after what they want from life) and then contrasting this bleak picture with action imagery (e.g. taking risks to create interesting/exciting opportunities, doing instead of stewing). Clients are asked to carry out this exercise on a daily basis for the next few weeks while gradually fading out the inaction imagery and keeping a diary to determine if the desired action is actually occurring.

Behavioural assignments include:

1   *Activity scheduling*. This is a technique used with depressed clients, particularly in the early stages of therapy, as it helps them to combat their inactivity, inertia, indecisiveness and rumination. Each day is usually divided into hourly periods of planned activity so clients do not have to decide every hour what to do next. Clients are asked to rate on a

0–10 scale how much pleasure and sense of accomplishment they have gained from each activity. This rating scale helps clients to test their predictions that carrying out these activities will bring neither pleasure nor accomplishment. Activity scheduling is a key behavioural activation technique used in the treatment of depression (Kuehlwein, 2002). Behavioural activation (BA) has become a treatment in its own right for depression rather than as an important component of a CBT programme (Martell *et al.*, 2010). BA is part of the third wave in CBT (see Point 100) which 're-emphasiz[es] behavioral principles and de-emphasiz[es] the *content* of cognition' (Craske, 2010: 2; emphasis in original).

2   *Graded task assignments.* These help clients to tackle their problems in small, manageable steps rather than attempting too much too soon. A hierarchy of feared or difficult situations can be drawn up with the client moving through the hierarchy at his own pace, culminating in him facing the most difficult or feared situation. For example, a person with a dog phobia watched a dog playing from a safe distance, then began to move closer until he was able to stroke a tethered dog before facing his ultimate fear of an untethered dog 'sniffing' around him. He was able to overcome his fear within a few days.

3   *Experiments.* These enable clients to test their thoughts and beliefs, to treat them as hypotheses rather than as facts. For example, a client believed that his heterosexual friends would drop him if he told them he was gay. He said he wanted to 'stop living a lie and come out into the open'. His announcement of his sexual orientation provoked a range of reactions: 'we knew', disbelief, support, wariness among some male friends, and a few did 'drop me'. The client's prediction was, to a large extent, not realized and he felt relieved by the outcome; but some difficulties now emerged, such as 'some of my male friends are worried that I might fancy them'. How he would handle these difficulties received therapeutic attention. If all the client's heterosexual friends had dropped him, then the therapist would have helped him to examine the quality of his pre-disclosure

relationships with them, find ways of accepting the grim reality of events and consider how he would approach forming future friendships with heterosexuals.

It is important for therapists to read the research literature on the efficacy of CBT homework assignments (e.g. Tompkins, 2004; Kazantzis *et al.*, 2005) and, based on what they have learnt from this undertaking, to develop a portfolio of effective between-session tasks for use with their clients.

65

NEGOTIATING HOMEWORK ASSIGNMENTS

Obvious as it may seem, negotiation is based on collaboration, not telling the clients what assignments to carry out (telling may occur, for example, because the therapist wants her client 'to feel good about himself' as quickly as possible as his rapid improvement will reflect her clinical competence). Homework assignments should be based on the work undertaken in the current session and linked to the client's goals, e.g. preparing an activity schedule in the session, then the client implementing it as homework in order to see if it raises his depressed mood. The homework task needs to be stated in clear and concrete terms (e.g. 'I will make three phone calls from home in the next week to enquire about college courses'), as well as when it will be done (e.g. 'On Monday, Wednesday and Friday mornings').

Anticipated obstacles to carrying out the assignment need to be identified (such as 'I might forget') and solutions developed ('I'll leave a note by the phone so I won't forget'). Clients can be given a copy of the completed homework form (see Appendix 3) in order to remind them of what they have agreed to do. Sufficient time (e.g. ten minutes) should be left at the end of the session for homework negotiation; if this process is rushed, misunderstandings may occur such as the client not having a clear understanding of what he is supposed to do as the assignment has been couched in vague terms. If an appropriate homework assignment has emerged earlier in the session it can be discussed and agreed upon then or nearer the end of the session.

Other considerations for the therapist to bear in mind are assessing whether the client has the skills to execute the assignment (e.g. the client wants to act assertively in a specific context but does not understand what assertive behaviour actually is; in-session rehearsal of assertive behaviour would be required) and does the task actually interest the client (e.g. the client may feel duty-bound to fill out DTR forms but an action assignment would be more stimulating for her). More experienced therapists may help clients to list several homework assignments from which they can choose the most interesting and relevant one (Padesky and Greenberger, 1995).

The therapist should point out to her clients that homework is based on a 'win–win' formula: this means that whatever happens with homework tasks, important information will be obtained. Thus, if the client completes the assignment, how was this accomplished? If the client carried out a task other than the agreed one, what happened to alter the task? If the client did not attempt the task, what prevented him from carrying it out? Homework is based on learning, not success or failure.

During the early stages of therapy, starting homework in the session (if possible) provides the fillip for clients to continue it outside of the session. As Beck observes: 'Patients often describe the hardest part of doing homework as the period *just before* they initiate it – that is, motivating themselves to get started' (2011: 302; emphasis in original). For example, I (MN) saw a client who was procrastinating over starting her dissertation for her university course. She agreed to start making notes in the session, cognitive blocks were identified ('I want to write a brilliant opening paragraph that will really impress my tutor') and tackled ('I'll start with an adequate opening paragraph, revise it when necessary, and leave the tutor to decide what he makes of it'). Writing assignments, imagery exercises or practising new behaviours can be initiated before the end of the session and any difficulties in carrying them out addressed.

As therapy progresses, the client should be suggesting homework assignments as part of her developing role as a self-therapist as this will encourage her to continue to devise and execute self-help assignments once formal therapy has ended. The client is less likely to do this if the therapist has played the major role in homework negotiation throughout the course of therapy.

66

REVIEWING HOMEWORK ASSIGNMENTS

Reviewing homework is usually the first item on the session agenda. Overlooking homework review creates three problems:

> First, the patients usually begin to think that the homework is not important and, therefore, that treatment is something done to them rather than something they actively work on even in the absence of the therapist. Second, the therapists miss opportunities to correct mistakes such as the patients inadequately responding rationally to their automatic thoughts. Third, the therapists lose the chance to draw helpful lessons from the homework and to reinforce these lessons.
>
> (Beck *et al.*, 1993: 109)

Tompkins (2004) suggests 5 Cs for reviewing homework tasks:

1 Be consistent – review the client's homework in every session.
2 Be curious – adopt an open-minded, non-judgemental approach to reviewing homework particularly if the client has not completed it.
3 Be complimentary – no matter how small the effort was in attempting to carry out the assignment.
4 Be careful – do not reinforce homework non-compliance by pretending it does not matter. Instead, examine the blocks that prevented task completion.
5 Consider changing or repeating the homework task depending on the information that has emerged from this examination.

A common problem is homework non-compliance. Persons (1989) suggests three common obstacles impeding homework completion: (1) perfectionism (e.g. 'If I can't do the task perfectly, then it's not worth bothering about'); (2) fear of failure (e.g. 'If I fail at the task, this will prove how useless I am'); and (3) the need to please others (e.g. 'I can't see the usefulness of the task the therapist has suggested but I'll say I'll try to do it because I don't want her to think badly of me').

Tackling these obstacles can start (1) with Hauck's assertion that 'it is more important to do than to do well ... think of success rather as a slight bit of improvement over what you were able to do before' (1982: 47); (2) point out that failing is a process while failure is the outcome, so a person can experience a number of failings at task completion but eventually succeed in carrying it out (Neenan and Dryden, 2002), and that the person may fail to execute a particular task but it is demonstrably false to say the person is a failure or useless because of it; and (3) encourage the client to voice her true reactions to the homework assignment and suggest one herself that she would find genuinely helpful.

Difficulties in executing homework assignments can be predicted from the client's case conceptualization (see Point 30). For example, a client who presents with procrastination problems is likely to put off carrying out his homework tasks. The therapist and client can devise an anti-procrastination plan to facilitate homework completion (e.g. to strengthen the client's motivation, he agrees to send an email to the therapist when the task is completed within the strict deadline). Of course, there is no guarantee the plan will work every time, but it may help to reduce the number of times homework tasks are not completed.

Padesky and Greenberger (1995) stress that the therapist should not see homework non-compliance as resistance to therapy but, instead, adopt a problem-solving outlook (e.g. 'Let's see if we can find out what's going on'). Trying to break down resistance can lead to power struggles or impasses in therapy while the working together approach is likely to produce helpful gains for the client and the therapeutic alliance.

Therapists need to monitor their own reactions to homework non-compliance such as feeling angry because the client is not 'taking therapy seriously' or feeling anxious because continuing non-compliance on the client's part will prove that the therapist is incompetent – 'If I was a good therapist, then I should have found a way to tackle this issue by now'. Through supervision and/or filling out a DTR form, the therapist can generate adaptive responses to his own automatic thoughts such as: 'It's better to probe for the reasons behind the client's non-compliance rather than attribute it to her not taking therapy seriously or my incompetence. I'll record my sessions with her and take them to supervision for a more objective look at what could be going on.'

67

REVEALING 'IF ... THEN' STATEMENTS

Identifying and examining underlying assumptions and rules (see Point 3) occurs when clients have gained some skill and confidence in applying the cognitive model to their problems by answering their situation-specific NATs and completing some homework assignments (working on NATs 'chips away' at underlying beliefs). Tackling deeper cognitive levels first, bypassing NATs, may result in clients feeling overwhelmed, threatened, overly defensive or resistant because the therapist has gone too deep, too soon – a strategy which might lead some clients to terminate therapy prematurely. Having said all that, we have worked with clients who were ready, willing and able to work on their rules of living and core beliefs early in therapy (e.g. 'I know what's at the root of my problems, so let's go straight there').

A key way to identify a cross-situational underlying assumption is for the therapist to be alert for client statements using an 'if ... then' construction such as 'If I don't do as I'm told, then my partner will leave me' (assumptions can also be expressed in an 'unless ... then' form such as 'Unless I'm always on top of things, then my life will become totally chaotic'). The terms of the assumption are set by the 'if ...'; the 'then ...' inflicts its punishment if these terms are not met. Fennell points out that 'sometimes the "if ... then ..." is not immediately obvious, but you will see it if you look carefully' (1999: 165). For example, a client says his motto is, 'Don't get close', but when deconstructed shows its 'if ... then' origins: 'If I get close to people, then they will reject me'; another client says that his policy is 'to keep one step ahead of the game', which when translated into assumptive form is, 'If I don't keep one step ahead of people by anticipating their actions, then I'll be used or exploited by them in some way.' Another way to elicit an 'if ... then' assumption is to provide the 'if ...' part of it:

Client: Why do I always massively overprepare for a presentation? Why can't I just do a reasonable amount of preparation?

Therapist: Let's find some answers to your questions. If I don't massively overprepare for a presentation ...

Client: Then I'll feel I don't really know my subject, give a poor presentation and lose my credibility.

Therapist: If I just do a reasonable amount of preparation ...

Client: Then I'll probably struggle with some of the questions and lose my credibility because I really don't know my subject. It's a credibility issue then. That's why I massively overprepare. I think I knew that already; saying it out loud just confirms it.

While we stress looking for maladaptive assumptions in an 'if/ unless ... then' form they can be expressed in many different forms, such as 'I don't deserve any happiness in life because of what I did', 'My worth is dependent on what others think of me' and 'Other people's needs are more important than mine'.

On a technical note, some 'if ...then' statements are actually situation-specific automatic thoughts (Beck, 2005), e.g. 'If I speak to Sue about the noise levels, she'll tell me to "get lost"' and 'If I ask John for a lift to the station, he'll say he hasn't got the time to do it'. Both of these predictions can be tested through behavioural experiments. These two and other situation-specific 'if ... then' statements coalesced into an underlying cross-situational assumption which, up to this point in the client's life, had remained unarticulated by her: 'If I try to speak up for myself and what I would like to happen, then no one pays any attention to me and treats me as insignificant [possible core belief].'

68

SPOTTING 'MUSTS' AND 'SHOULDS'

These are imperative statements driving the client's behaviour, such as 'I must always perform perfectly' and 'I should never let my friends down'. These rules are maladaptive because they are rigid, do not allow for human fallibility (imperfection) or changes in circumstances. Must and should statements 'usually link up with a hidden "or else"' (Fennell, 1999: 166) which the therapist helps to make explicit by asking: 'Is there an "or else" attached to those statements?' With the above examples, the 'or else' is, respectively, 'I'll become a mediocrity' and 'They will all desert me'. Clients can learn to spot the 'musts' and 'shoulds' in their thinking once the therapist points out their disturbance-inducing importance:

Client: I shouldn't forget to phone my mother. I should phone her when I say I will. I feel very guilty when I don't phone her.

Therapist: You did say you have a very demanding job as well as a family to look after. Do you make any allowances for that?

Client: No. That should not make any difference. I shouldn't forget to phone my mother.

Therapist: Are you aware that you've used the word 'should' four times in your last two sentences?

Client: What of it?

Therapist: The word 'should' can act like a slave driver dictating to you what you should and should not do. Does that strike any chords in you?

Client: [nodding] It's true I do drive myself pretty hard. My head is like a pressure cooker sometimes. I do use that word a lot.

163

> *Therapist*:   Would you like to keep a diary for the next week and see how many 'shoulds' you can spot in your thinking?
>
> *Client*:   Okay. That should be interesting. [laughs]

The client's 'or else' statement attached to 'I shouldn't forget to phone my mother' was 'this will prove that I am an uncaring daughter'. If the client is receptive, the therapist can inject some humour into this process of spotting shoulds and musts by asking her client: 'Have you been engaging in some S and M in the last week?'

It is important to point out that not all must and should statements uttered by clients require clinical scrutiny: the therapist's important task is to help her clients to discriminate between the various meanings embedded in these words, e.g. 'It should snow tomorrow according to the weather forecast' (prediction), 'I must lose some weight soon' (intention), 'You should read that book, it's so funny' (recommendation), and 'I must wash my hair tonight as my scalp is getting rather itchy' (understandable). Only rigid and unrelenting musts and shoulds are targeted for discussion such as 'I must win every argument I engage in'. If the therapist does not teach these differences in meaning, some clients might believe that all musts and shoulds are toxic, e.g. 'I must never say "must".'

DISCERNING THEMES IN CLIENTS' AUTOMATIC THOUGHTS

The therapist can review with her client his Daily Thought Records (DTRs) in a range of situations in order to help him become aware of a particular theme(s) that may be recurring in his thinking. For example, a sample of the client's thought records at home, work and in social situations are, respectively, 'Everything has to be just right', 'I need to ensure that my colleagues see me in the way I want to be seen' and 'I can't enjoy myself without the right people around me'. The therapist can ask him if he recognizes a theme running through these thoughts or whether he can infer a particular rule or assumption underpinning them:

Client: I'm not sure what you mean.
Therapist: In doing this exercise with other clients, themes of rejection, failure, or approval have been identified.
Client: I'm still not sure.
Therapist: Well, in going over these thought forms there seems to be the need for control in your life. Is that the case?
Client: I think that's true. I like everything to be the way I want it to be.
Therapist: And if everything is not the way you want it to be …?
Client: Then I think my life is out of control, falling apart. [the client's assumption has been revealed]

INVESTIGATING MARKED MOOD VARIATIONS

Fennell suggests that 'high mood often indicates that the terms of an assumption have been met, just as low mood signals its violation' (1989: 204). Clients can investigate their high moods as well as their low ones in order to uncover important information about their assumptions and rules. Beck *et al.* suggest that when a client feels particularly happy about an event 'questions about his thinking may lead to his base rules. Many of the dysfunctional formulas "pay off" for the patient when they appear to be working' (1979: 249). For example, a client said that she felt absolutely delighted that her boss had given her a 'well done' for bringing in an important project on time – 'I was floating on a cloud all day'. The therapist probed to discover the reasons behind the client's elated mood:

> *Client*: It feels great, I feel great. My self-esteem went sky high. I like being praised. Who doesn't?
>
> *Therapist*: What does it mean to you to receive praise?
>
> *Client*: That I'm liked and considered a worthwhile person.
>
> *Therapist*: What do you have to do or be in order to be liked and considered worthwhile?
>
> *Client*: I have to do my best to please others.
>
> *Therapist*: So would you say that you act in accordance with the following assumption: 'If I do my best to please others, then they will like me and consider me a worthwhile person'?
>
> *Client*: That sounds right. My boss praised me, I felt good. What's wrong with that?

However, her high mood did not last for long as her boss was critical of her a few days later when she was late for a meeting: 'I felt destroyed when he criticized me. A few days ago he had nothing but praise for me.' The negative assumption, the flip side of the positive one, triggered the client's depressed mood: 'If I fail to please others, then they will condemn and reject me.' Clients can keep a diary to monitor these marked mood variations to help them discover what assumptions and rules they subscribe to.

71

THE DOWNWARD ARROW

This is a technique used to uncover underlying beliefs such as assumptions, rules and core beliefs (Burns, 1999). As Beck *et al.* observe:

> Many patients are unable to articulate these underlying beliefs until they have been asked to consider the personal *meaning* that their more manifest thoughts have for them. Therefore, when patients exhibit strong negative emotions that seem to be far more intense than their automatic thoughts alone would cause, therapists can ask patients to probe a bit deeper by asking successive variations of the question "What does that *mean* to you?"
>
> (1993: 140; emphases in original)

By pursuing the personal meaning of hot (emotionally charged) thoughts, the therapist helps the client to peel back layers of thought until an underlying belief is revealed. The downward arrow locates the cognitive source of this strong emotion. Unlike responding to automatic thoughts, each thought uncovered in the downward arrow is accepted as temporarily true until a belief is revealed. (If the thoughts were challenged as they appeared this would undermine the downward arrow technique as the client's attention would be directed elsewhere thereby leaving maladaptive underlying beliefs intact.) In the following example, a client is very anxious about going out with a new boyfriend and puts it down to the thought that 'He's bound not to fancy me':

Therapist: Let's assume he doesn't fancy you, then what?

↓

Client: I'm back on the shelf.

Therapist: And if you are back on the shelf, why would that be upsetting to you?

↓

Client: Isn't it obvious?

Therapist: I need to hear it from you rather than make a guess myself, so why would that be upsetting to you?

↓

Client: Because no one wants me.

Therapist: And if that's true, what would that mean to you?

↓

Client: That I'll always be alone, stuck on the shelf.

Therapist: To sum up then: do you believe that 'If no one wants me, then I'll always be alone, stuck on the shelf'?

Client: Yes, that's what I believe. [client's assumption is revealed and confirmed]

Beck points out that 'asking what a thought means *to* the patient often elicits an intermediate belief [rule/assumption]; asking what it means *about* the patient usually uncovers the core belief' (2011: 207; emphases in original). Uncovering core beliefs through the use of the downward arrow is demonstrated in Point 81.

MEMORIES, FAMILY SAYINGS, MOTTOES

Fennell observes that 'rules have their roots in experience. Sometimes people can trace them back to particular early memories, or to sayings that were current in the household where they grew up. Identifying these may help you to understand the policies you have adopted' (1999: 170). For example, a client remembered her parents telling her not to 'get above yourself' when 'I started to sing my own praises or feel good about myself'. The client said she still remembers and follows her parents' injunction which stops her from taking pride in her achievements or enjoying the praise of others as this would mean 'I'm being conceited'. Another client said he had 'perfectionists as parents' who pushed their children to be the best at everything they did: 'The family motto was "Always be first".' While following this motto had helped the client to achieve considerable success in life through relentless determination, the physical and psychological costs of such determination were also considerable.

Recognizing voices from the past also includes those of teachers, friends and relatives. For example, a client said that he felt guilty if he took time out from his busy life to enjoy himself: 'I should be able to relax, have a laugh from time to time. What's wrong with that?' However, 'having a laugh' had associations in his mind with idleness and wasted time. When the therapist asked him if these associations were echoes from the past, he said that a schoolteacher he had greatly respected had frequently told him that 'Idleness was only to be tolerated in the grave. Don't waste a moment of your life'. The client had absorbed this message which had resulted in his 'maximize-every-moment' lifestyle and feelings of guilt when time was being 'wasted'.

BEHAVIOURAL EXPERIMENTS

In this point and the following ones (74–80), ways of revising underlying assumptions and rules will be discussed. Assumptions are best tested with behavioural experiments (Padesky and Greenberger, 1995). The 'If …' part of the assumption can be put to the test in order to determine if the 'then …' part will be realized. For example, a client believed 'If I say what I want, then others will see me as selfish and reject me'. As an experiment, on a night out with her girlfriends, the client stated what film she wanted to see and where she wanted to eat afterwards. To her surprise, her friends agreed and asked her why she did not speak up more often. She spoke up on several more occasions to test further her assumption with, again, no adverse consequences (though her friends did not always go along with her wishes). The client's reformulated assumption was: 'If I say what I want, then others will see it as normal behaviour but not always agree to do what I want.'

Another client thought: 'If I speak up in a group, then I'll say something stupid and everyone will laugh at me.' The client was anxious about carrying out this experiment and wanted reassurance that nothing bad would happen, but the therapist pointed out that if the outcome was known before it had occurred then it was not an experiment. The client did speak up in the group and stumbled over some of her words, which elicited some titters from a few group members. The client concluded from the experiment that her assumption had been proved correct. However, the majority of group members did not laugh, stumbling over her words is not a mark of stupidity (unless the client believes that it is) but a sign of her nervousness, and what laughter there was can be dismissed as insensitive unless, again, the client sees it as further confirmation of her stupidity.

Reviewing the outcome of a behavioural experiment needs to be carefully carried out to avoid either the client or therapist jumping to conclusions. After such a detailed discussion, the client decided on a new and self-helping alternative to her old dysfunctional assumption: 'When I speak up in groups, my focus will be on learning and self-acceptance, not seeing myself as stupid or paying attention to others' laughter if I get things wrong.' Fennell suggests that 'alternatives to dysfunctional assumptions can be written on flash-cards for patients to read repeatedly until acting in accordance with them becomes second nature' (1989: 207).

Behavioural experiments can be used straight away to test the usefulness of clients' new rules and assumptions instead of being used first to test the validity of the old ones. Mooney and Padesky (2000) suggest a number of advantages if the focus is on constructing new rules and assumptions:

1 Changes occur more quickly.
2 The collaborative process is creative rather than revisionist, i.e. creating new possibilities, not modifying old thinking traps.
3 Client motivation and interest are increased.
4 More change may occur if a panorama of possibilities is considered instead of the constricted vision offered by focusing on old patterns of behaviour.

Having said all that, the therapist should discuss with her clients the different ways behavioural experiments can be used rather than assume they all want them to be creative rather than revisionist (therapists' enthusiastic thinking about the changes clients could be making often overlooks the wariness inherent in clients' thinking about change).

Not all assumptions can be tested with behavioural experiments to determine if the client's prediction is accurate, e.g. 'If I'm bad in this life, then I will suffer in the afterlife'. How can the 'then …' part of the assumption be tested? With this assumption, the therapist would want to know what the client means by 'bad': deliberately acting badly or the inevitable transgressions of a fallible human being? Will the client experience ceaseless suffering or will it be time-limited? Is the client's God compassionate or vengeful? Could the client be rewarded rather than punished in the afterlife? Through such discussions, the therapist is attempting to help the client construct a balanced view of what awaits him in the afterlife rather than his fixation on fire and brimstone.

Unable to test the 'then …' part of the assumption, the client is able to carry out another kind of behavioural experiment which is to conduct a survey (see Point 59) among the knowledgeable in religious matters to ascertain their views on the subject. As a result of the survey, the client said he found someone more 'authoritative and understanding' than the therapist to talk to about his worries and left therapy (the therapist told his supervisor that he struggled to sustain a conversation about the afterlife as he had no interest in religion).

74

DISOBEYING THE 'SHOULDS' AND 'MUSTS'

Rules of living are often expressed in rigid should and must statements such as 'I should never let anyone down' or 'I must always be strong and capable'. One way to modify these rules is by disobeying them to determine if the implicit and unpleasant 'or else' attached to the rule will be realized ('I must always be strong and capable or else I will be despised if I show weakness and indecisiveness'). For example, a client's rule was: 'I should put in consistently long hours at the office or else my colleagues will see me as a slacker and I'll lose their respect.' She agreed to vary her hours at the office and came in later on some days and went home earlier on other days. To her surprise, most of her colleagues complimented her on 'starting to look after yourself instead of overdoing it', and stated that they never had regarded her as a slacker and it would take something very serious to occur for them to lose their respect for her; a few colleagues commented that they did not know nor were they interested in how many hours she worked as they were too busy with their own work (which helped to correct the client's overestimation of how much attention was paid to her and how much respect she had).

Revising rigid rules means making them reasonable and flexible. The client's new rule was: 'I don't mind working long hours when it's necessary, but not in order to try and influence the way my colleagues see me. I'll leave it up to them to decide whether or not I have their respect. I want to do my best at work rather than have to keep on proving myself to my colleagues.' As well as reasonable and flexible, new rules are often lengthy and elaborate in stark contrast to the all-or-nothing quality of the old rules: 'This reflects the fact that they are based on an adult's ability to understand how the world works at a deeper level and to take account of variations in circumstances' (Fennell, 1999: 183). Such a lengthy new rule can prove mentally cumbersome and be one which the client might 'trip over' when trying to remember or rehearse it, so the therapist can suggest that the client should construct a pithy version of it such as: 'Be myself, not prove myself, at work' (which the client eventually extended to other areas of her life where she believed she must not lose the respect of others).

75

REDRAWING PERSONAL CONTRACTS

Assumptions and rules can be viewed as contracts that clients have drawn up with themselves (Blackburn and Davidson, 1995). For example, a client's contract was, 'If I help my friends, then they should help me'; however, the terms of the contract were often unfulfilled as some of her friends did not help her when she requested it which left her feeling bitterly disappointed by her friends' 'betrayal'. David Burns pinpoints what is wrong with these contracts – they assume a natural reciprocity: 'Reciprocity is a transient and inherently unstable ideal that can only be approximated through continued effort. This involves mutual consensus, communication, compromise, and growth. It requires negotiation and hard work' (1999: 174). The client did not understand this important point and assumed that her friends instinctively knew the terms of her contract, but the reality was that the contract was unilateral, not bilateral; therefore it was invalid.

In order to stop feeling bitterly disappointed when some of her friends let her down, the client decided to rewrite her personal contract in more reasonable and realistic terms: 'When I help my friends, which I like to do, I will no longer automatically expect them to help me in return though it would be nice if they helped me sometimes.' Another client, who had recently lost his job, believed passionately in his unilateral contract, 'As I desperately want another job, then I should be given one'; unfortunately, each job interview failed to gain him one and he started despairing at the 'unfairness of it all'. The client was overlooking a simple fact: job applicants are picked for their skills and talents pertaining to the job, not on the basis of their desperation or deservingness for one. The client rewrote his contract to reflect this fact: 'I very much want a job but no one has to give me one. I will keep on applying and making sure that my skills are appropriate for the jobs I go for. Every time I don't get the job I will ask for feedback to help me improve my interview skills.' The client was eventually successful at his eleventh job interview.

76

EXAMINING THE SHORT- AND LONG-TERM USEFULNESS OF ASSUMPTIONS AND RULES

Clients often focus on the immediate benefits to be derived from subscribing to a particular assumption or rule and are reluctant to look at its longer-term harmful effects; after all, why should they bother looking ahead when their assumptions or rules are currently producing good results for them? Beck *et al.* state that this is precisely the time to examine these assumptions and rules:

> Many who believe that they need the approval of everyone are often extremely happy when they think they have this approval. Others who believe their value depends on their performance are often overjoyed when they are performing well. The job of the therapist is to help the patient see *the long-term effects* of operating under these rules.
>
> (Beck *et al.*, 1979: 270; emphasis in original)

Clients who believe they need the approval of others in order to feel good about themselves are putting control over their feelings into others' hands (whether these others realize it or not): approval puts their mood up and disapproval brings it down. It is important for 'approval-seekers' to look ahead in order to see the emotional distress they are likely to experience when approval is withdrawn and to start constructing more helpful assumptions and rules that do not make their self-worth conditional, such as: 'It's very nice to have people's approval, but it's not essential and it's unlikely to last. Better to develop self-acceptance which means I don't have to look to others in order to feel good about myself. Self-acceptance can be a constant factor in my life, approval from others usually isn't.' Those clients who link self-value to a particular performance can break this link by seeing the self as unrateable, only the performance is rateable: 'Whether my performance is good, bad or indifferent has no bearing on me as a person. I will learn to focus on evaluating the particular performance, not evaluating myself on the basis of it.'

77

DEVELOPING AN ALTERNATIVE ASSUMPTION THAT RETAINS THE ADVANTAGES OF THE MALADAPTIVE ASSUMPTION AND JETTISONS ITS DISADVANTAGES

Maladaptive assumptions are often constructed in rigid and extreme terms such as 'If I don't always maintain my high standards, then this will prove I'm incompetent'. The client never felt any real enjoyment when he did maintain his standards because he was always worried about falling below them and became depressed when he did. The client acknowledged the need to modify this assumption but feared that in so doing his high standards would drop sharply: 'I know it sounds strange, but it motivates me to think that way and it's given me quite a bit of success':

Therapist: Your modified assumption would aim to keep the success and motivation but give up the self-downing and thereby avoid experiencing the depression that flows from it.

Client: It sounds good put like that but how do I actually change it?

Therapist: Well, look at the 'If ...' part of your assumption, what's the troublesome word there?

Client: 'Always'. There's no leeway for allowing myself to fall below my high standards because I do sometimes.

Therapist: And no compassion or understanding when you do. Look at the 'then …' part of your assumption.

Client: I worry that if I drop the 'always', then my standards will collapse into mediocrity.

Therapist: You've just stated another assumption and you need to put that to the test as well. You're investing the word 'always' with an almost mystical power. It has no power independently of you. You can deprive it of power if you stop believing in it and think of a non-extreme alternative that will lead to a different and compassionate conclusion when you fall below your standards. What sounds like a reasonable alternative to you?

Client: Okay. I really do want to maintain my high standards but … hmm.

Therapist: That's a start.

After further discussion with the therapist, the client's new assumption, which kept the helpful parts of the old assumption and ditched the unhelpful parts, was: 'I really do want to maintain my high standards but when I fall below them, as I have done already, I will not condemn myself as incompetent. Instead, I will accept what has happened and see what I can do to put it right.' Obviously, verbalizing a new assumption in the therapist's office carries little conviction unless the client repeatedly and forcefully acts in support of it in a variety of situations where the old maladaptive assumption was operative. By the end of therapy, the client had experienced several occasions where he fell below his high standards (they did not collapse into mediocrity) and focused on 'what went wrong and putting it right' instead of self-condemnation. He said that the time he previously wasted 'on feeling bad and putting myself down' was now channelled into productive problem-solving.

78

LISTING THE ADVANTAGES AND DISADVANTAGES OF A RULE OR ASSUMPTION

Clients can be encouraged to list and examine the advantages and disadvantages of holding a particular rule or assumption (see Point 53 for using this technique with automatic thoughts). In the following example, the client's assumption was written on the whiteboard in the therapist's office and the board was divided into two columns:

ASSUMPTION: 'IF I'M NOT IN CONTROL OF MY FEELINGS, THEN I'LL BECOME UNSTABLE AND HYSTERICAL'

Advantages	Disadvantages
1 'It keeps me emotionally strong'	1 'I feel emotionally repressed as well'
2 'People admire my sangfroid'	2 'It's often an act I put on for people because I'm scared of revealing how I really feel'
3 'To be honest, I feel superior to those who are an emotional mess'	3 'Feelings of superiority don't last for long. I begin to wonder who really is the emotional mess – them or me?'

4 'Other people can express
their feelings without
becoming unstable and
hysterical. I'm not giving
myself the chance to
experiment with my
feelings'

5 'I sometimes don't even
allow myself to laugh too
much in case people think
I'm getting hysterical'

As usually happens with this technique, the disadvantages eventually outweigh the advantages (though the therapist may need to prompt some clients to focus on the disadvantages as they more readily list the advantages than the drawbacks of their rules and assumptions). Clients can also be asked to re-examine the advantages in order to determine how advantageous they really are:

Therapist: Do you actually feel emotionally strong?
Client: Not really. A friend of mine can laugh or cry when the mood takes him. He's not worried what others think of him. That's true strength. I'm always worried what others would think of me if I was spontaneous with my feelings. I'm trying to control them all the time. I'm the real emotional mess.
Therapist: It doesn't have to stay that way.

With the disadvantages outweighing the advantages and some of the advantages revealed as self-defeating, clients are then likely to initiate change and thereby generate more functional assumptions, such as in the above example: 'I would like to experiment with my feelings rather than always holding back, pretending to be in control. I don't believe any longer that expressing my feelings, when it is appropriate, will lead to instability or hysteria but, instead, I hope will lead to a richer emotional life that I have denied myself for so long.' The client can now, with this assumption, explore new possibilities for himself such as laughing uproariously when he finds something very funny compared with previously allowing himself only a mild titter in order to maintain self-control in the company of others.

79

EXPLORING THE HISTORICAL DEVELOPMENT OF ASSUMPTIONS AND RULES

Fennell suggests that 'understanding how dysfunctional assumptions were formed promotes distance from them' (1989: 206) and consequently a more dispassionate evaluation of them can be conducted. This development usually starts early in life (but not inevitably so) as children form their assumptions and rules in the light of their experiences and relationships with others; these assumptions and rules help them to make sense of the world around them. For example, a child who is harshly criticized by her parents when she is naughty – 'You're a little devil. No one will ever like you if you don't behave yourself' – does her best to 'be good' thereafter. 'Be good' eventually becomes an unarticulated assumption: 'Unless I please others, they'll criticize me and then reject me as unlikeable.' While this 'be good' strategy may have been adaptive for the child in order to avoid parental anger and criticism, as an adult it has become maladaptive as the client is submissive in her relationships (home, work and social) and 'lives' too much in the minds of others ('I'm always wondering what people think of me. Do they like me? Have I upset them in some way? It's ridiculous but I can't seem to stop doing it').

By comparing and contrasting the operation of the assumption in childhood and adulthood, the client came to the conclusion that it had outlived its usefulness ('It's exhausting always trying to please others and worrying about whether they like me or not') and led her to developing a moderate and self-helping assumption: 'I still want to please others at times but not because I feel I have to. I will also start pleasing myself and speaking up for me. If I get criticized or rejected for it, too bad. I am likeable despite what others might think.' As always, a new rule or assumption is only theoretical when voiced in the therapist's office, so if it is to be internalized it needs to be put into daily practice in the client's life.

The client discovered that she greatly overestimated being criticized by others when she stood up for herself, and what criticism she did encounter enabled her to test the strength of her new belief that she was indeed likeable despite what some people might think of her ('I don't get all sort of crumbly and wobbly inside like I used to when I thought someone didn't like me'). One of the most pleasurable changes she described was 'moving out of the minds of others and spending much more time in my own mind enjoying my own interests'. As dysfunctional rules and assumptions are usually long-standing, Fennell cautions that 'it could take as much as six to eight months for your new rule to take over completely. As long as the new rule is useful to you and you can see it taking you in useful and interesting directions, don't give up' (1999: 187).

80

USING IMAGERY TO MODIFY ASSUMPTIONS

In Point 58 we looked at using imagery to modify NATs. Here we look at using imagery to revise dysfunctional assumptions. For example, an anxious client who has distressing images of fainting in the high street and being laughed at never gets beyond in her mind the 'fainting and the laughter'. Her assumption is: 'If I faint in public, then people will laugh at me and call me a drunk' ('in public' referred to a variety of situations such as shops, railway station and the public library). The therapist guides the client beyond the 'fainting and the laughter' to arrive at a different interpretation of the situation:

Therapist: Close your eyes and imagine you have fainted in the high street. What's happening now?

Client: I'm unconscious. People are pointing and laughing at me and saying 'She's a drunk'.

Therapist: How will you know what people are doing or saying if you're unconscious?

Client: That's true. I never thought of that.

Therapist: How long do you think you will be unconscious for?

Client: Only a couple of minutes.

Therapist: What do you see when you open your eyes? Anyone laughing?

Client: No. They're asking me if I'm okay and shall they call an ambulance.

Therapist: Can you hear anyone calling you a 'drunk' or anything else?

Client: I can't hear that. People are concerned for my welfare, helping me to my feet and picking up my handbag for me.

Therapist: What happens then?

Client: People say goodbye. I thank them for helping me and then they go about their business which my fainting interrupted. I walk home, a little bit unsteady on my feet but I feel okay by the time I get home.

Therapist: How are you feeling now about fainting in public?

Client: Much less worried.

Therapist: What's changed for you then?

Client: Well, if I faint in the high street, then people are much more likely to help me than laugh at me or call me a 'drunk'. [new assumption] It does seem a more realistic picture of how people will react. [client opens her eyes]

Therapist: Have you ever seen anyone faint?

Client: Yes I have. I saw someone faint in the shopping centre a few years ago and lots of people went to his aid. I don't know why I think people will be nasty to me. Do you know?

Therapist: We can discuss that later in the session, okay? [client nods] With this imagery exercise, you'll need to practise it regularly in order to strengthen in your mind this realistic outcome.

Client: I can see the sense in that.

This time a projection exercise (Lazarus, 1984) enabled the client to construct a new assumption based on a realistic appraisal of the likely reaction of others to her predicament which was reinforced by her own recollections of public reaction to a person who had fainted. If the client had wanted to include in the imagery exercise someone calling her a 'drunk', the therapist could have asked her: 'Who has accurate knowledge about you: you or a complete stranger?' With regard to the client's query why people would respond with nastiness towards her if she fainted, it emerged that she had been treated badly in earlier relationships and she saw such behaviour 'as the natural state of affairs in my life, so why would people treat me any differently if I fainted?'

81

THE DOWNWARD ARROW

When NATs have been answered, and dysfunctional rules and assumptions modified, core beliefs become the next target of therapeutic intervention (if this is clinically justified – see Point 16). Core beliefs are fundamental appraisals we make of ourselves (e.g. 'I'm not good enough'), others (e.g. 'You can't trust anyone') and the world (e.g. 'Everything is against me'). These are examples of maladaptive core beliefs – rigid and overgeneralized – which cognitive behavioural therapists help their clients to uncover. In this and the following points, (82–84), ways of revealing core beliefs are demonstrated. The downward arrow (demonstrated in Point 71 to uncover a client's underlying assumption) pursues the personal meaning for the client of each thought elicited until a core belief is revealed. It is important that the therapist does not engage in challenging the client's thoughts as this will prevent the 'arrow' from going 'down' very far. Nor should she ask long-winded questions that will distract the client from the often intense introspective focus required of him for the successful completion of this exercise, or insert her own interpretations of the client's problems into her questions (e.g. 'It seems to me that what you're really saying is that you're not a successful person. What does it mean to you to be an unsuccessful person?'). In the following example, the client is very worried about her husband's sudden willingness to stay late at work:

Therapist: What's anxiety-provoking for you about that?

↓

Client: He might be having an affair.

Therapist: And if he is having an affair, what then?

↓

Client: Well he's going to run off with the bitch.

Therapist: And if he does run off with the 'bitch' … ?

↓

Client: [becoming tearful] I'll be all alone, unwanted.

Therapist: What does that mean about you if you are all alone, unwanted.

↓

(Asking clients 'What does that mean about you?' rather than 'to you?' usually reveals a core belief – see Point 71.)

Client: That I'm unattractive, repulsive. [core belief]

In the above example the client was 'very worried' about her husband's behaviour. As Padesky observes: 'Questioning the meaning of high affect [emotion] events will usually quickly lead to the identification of schemas [core beliefs]' (1994: 269).

82

CONJUNCTIVE PHRASING

This refers to the therapist's use of phrases such as 'and that would mean …', 'and if that were true …' or 'and then …' to 'nudge along' her client's train of thought to its cognitive destination (i.e. core belief) by inviting him to finish his thoughts (DiGiuseppe, 1991b). The therapist removes the full stop at the end of the client's sentence and replaces it with a conjunction as in the following example:

Client:　　I might mess up things badly on my first date.
Therapist:　And if you did … ?
Client:　　It would be a disaster.
Therapist:　And that would mean…?
Client:　　That I'm a total dork. [core belief]

DiGiuseppe observes that an 'advantage of this method is that it keeps clients focused on their thoughts. The less a therapist says, the less clients have to respond to the therapist's words or attend to whether the therapist has understood them. The conjunctive phrase focuses clients on the meaning of their statements' (1991b: 168). We have used the term 'verbal economy' to convey the same point as DiGiuseppe's (Neenan and Dryden, 2000).

Sometimes a client's idiosyncratic usage needs investigating in order to tease out the core belief embedded within it, e.g. 'dipstick' means 'I'm stupid', and 'I'm an underwhelming kind of guy' translates as 'I'm boring'. The client's term a 'total dork' translated as 'absolutely hopeless with women'. This core belief reflected an aspect of the self (relationships with women) rather than commenting on or condemning the whole self. When a client says, for example, he is 'useless', the therapist needs to discover how widespread or limited is the operation of this belief in the client's life rather than jumping to conclusions about its presumed pervasiveness in his life.

SENTENCE COMPLETION

As core beliefs are usually stated in global terms, the therapist can write on her whiteboard or flipchart the following incomplete sentences and ask the client to 'fill in the blanks' in order to identify his core beliefs about himself, others and the world:

- I am ... powerless
- People are ... threatening
- The world is ... dangerous

This simple technique can prove very helpful for clients with limited intellectual and verbal abilities. Another example of sentence completion would be for the client to reveal a core belief aided by the therapist's prompting:

> *Client*: I'm scared stiff about the workshop going horribly wrong.
>
> *Therapist*: You're scared stiff about the workshop going horribly wrong because ... ?
>
> *Client*: That will prove to the world I'm a phoney. [core belief] I have no ability or skill to run a workshop.

Sentence completion falls just short of directly asking the client what her core beliefs are. Asking the client is the most straightforward way of eliciting core beliefs and should not be overlooked just because the therapist favours more sophisticated techniques like the downward arrow to display his clinical skill. In our experience, some clients know what their core beliefs are and will readily tell the therapist when asked, so textbook techniques will not be needed in these cases.

CORE BELIEFS APPEARING AS AUTOMATIC THOUGHTS

As we have said in earlier points, NATs are usually the first target of therapeutic intervention in CBT as they are the easiest level of thought to modify in order to bring symptomatic relief to clients. However, the therapist may run into trouble in attempting to modify a particular NAT because she is actually struggling with a core belief, not an automatic thought. Maybe the therapist's lack of knowledge or experience has contributed to this oversight or she believes that the client will automatically know what automatic thoughts are when she has explained them to him! In the following example, the client's core belief is 'hidden' in her outpouring of automatic thoughts but is detected by the therapist:

Therapist: What thoughts were going through your mind when you were told by your boss you were being made redundant?

Client: Bloody hell! Not again. You work your backside off and this is how things turn out. I deserve better than this. The boss was very impersonal about it: basically, clear your desk and then you're out. Wham-bam thank you ma'am. How am I supposed to pay the mortgage? Struggle, struggle, struggle, that's all I seem to do. 'Why bother?' I ask myself. I'm a failure [core belief], that's the reason. The whole process starts again: trudging around for another job, more soul-destroying interviews. I know, who said life was easy. I just wish it was sometimes. I don't know … things just seem to keep going wrong for me.

Therapist: Sounds like pretty bad times for you, but before we look at these issues in greater depth can I bring your attention to something you said – 'I'm a failure'. Is this a central view you have of yourself or is it just related to your current job difficulties?

Client: I'm not sure really. When times are bad I suppose I do see myself as a failure but when things are okay, I see myself as okay, normal. Thinking about it now though, I do see myself as more of a failure more of the time than seeing myself as okay.

Therapist: Would you want to focus now on the 'I'm a failure' belief or leave it to later in therapy?

Client: No, leave it to later. It's losing my job and having to find another one I want to talk about. That's the major hassle in my life at the moment.

When a core belief is revealed at the stage of identifying automatic thoughts, the therapist wants to ascertain if the client realizes she has revealed a core belief and knows of its presumed importance in maintaining her emotional problems; and if she does realize its importance, is she ready, willing and able to work on it now or does she want to postpone schema (core belief) work until she has acquired some CBT skills by working first on her surface thoughts. Generally speaking, schema work is usually carried out later rather than earlier in CBT because 'it is thought that challenging a patient's [core] beliefs too early in therapy will be counter-productive as the patient may feel threatened and resist change' (Blackburn and Davidson, 1995: 82). However, with clients who have personality disorders, the identification and modification of long-standing rigid core beliefs (e.g. 'I'm bad') starts early in therapy as these beliefs are activated in a wide range of situations and are the near-permanent outlook of such clients. As Davidson says: 'Core beliefs are the automatic thoughts in personality disorder!' (2008: 45).

85

EDUCATING CLIENTS ABOUT CORE BELIEFS

Educating clients about core beliefs (or schemas) serves as a prelude to modifying them. Core beliefs are usually formed in the light of early learning experiences; however, they can be recently formed, e.g. a person who prides herself on being strong and resourceful condemns herself as 'weak and helpless' for being unable to 'bounce back' into a busy lifestyle following a car crash. Core beliefs can be both positive (e.g. 'I'm likeable') and negative ('I'm unlikeable'); most people have both. Core beliefs process incoming information and thereby determine how we perceive events; in a sense, we can only see what the core belief allows us to. Dormant negative core beliefs are often activated and thereby pass into our awareness at times of emotional distress, such as a client who becomes depressed following the end of his marriage as he believes 'I'm worthless without her'. With this belief dominant in his thinking, any information or experience that contradicts his schema is likely to be dismissed, distorted or overlooked; the client will more actively process information that confirms this belief.

For example, the client is reluctant to accept any reassurances from his friends that he is still valued by them as this discrepant information would not 'fit' with his view of himself as worthless but, instead, focuses on information that would 'fit' with it: 'If I'm still valued so much by them, why are they coming round to see me less and less since my wife left me? They are lying.' Clients can also be asked what different life paths they might have taken with a more positive core belief guiding them, and how they see their future with this new belief beginning to take hold. For some clients this information can be a revelation as they now see that life has not arbitrarily 'picked on me to make me suffer' but that the path taken in life reflects their particular beliefs.

There are three main maladaptive behavioural responses used to cope with negative schemas (Young *et al.*, 2003):

1   Surrender – the person accepts the belief is true (e.g. 'I'm second best') and acts in accordance with it by not expecting much from his life or pushing himself to succeed.
2   Avoidance – the person avoids situations that might trigger the belief and the unpleasant emotions connected with it (e.g. parties, in case no one speaks to him).
3   Overcompensation – the person fights back against the belief in order to prove he is not second best (e.g. starts his own business).

Clients may exhibit all three behavioural responses, but with some more prominent than others (e.g. surrender and avoidance). Core belief education does not have to be too detailed or drawn-out, e.g. a client who sees herself as stupid is told by the therapist (with examples to illustrate his point) that she repeatedly thinks and acts in ways that confirm her 'stupidity'; in order to stop confirming this belief, she needs to think and act in support of a new, positive and flexible core belief yet to be developed (which would be the next step): 'That's easy to understand but will it be easy to change my belief? It looks pretty daunting after all these years and I'm a little frightened to be honest.' The therapist could reply, 'It will require some hard work and risk-taking but changed it certainly can be.'

While schema change can seem full of intriguing possibilities, for some clients there are just too many worrying unknowns about what these changes might involve for themselves and others and decide to leave therapy at this point:

> The therapist needs to respect the decision made by the patient and follow his or her lead in terms of whether to pursue schema change. In my experience, many patients look over the "precipice"

of schema change and choose not to make the leap and follow it through to its conclusion because of the perceived riskiness of the consequences.

(Dobson, 2012: 86)

Progress in therapy can be reviewed to this point, schema change remains an option if the client returns to therapy at a later date, and therapy can end with a feeling of mutual satisfaction with what has been achieved instead of a sense of failure that the client has 'shirked' the challenge of schema change and the therapist was not skilful enough to encourage her to undertake it.

86

DEVELOPING ALTERNATIVE CORE BELIEFS

As soon as clients' key core beliefs have been identified and schema education has begun, it is important for the client to start developing new and adaptive core beliefs. Mooney and Padesky (2000) advise that these new beliefs should be stated in the client's own words – they do not have to be the thematic opposite of the old core belief (e.g. 'I'm incompetent' versus 'I'm competent' or 'I'm worthless' versus 'I'm worthwhile'), and that the main focus of clinical attention is on constructing and strengthening new beliefs rather than on modifying old maladaptive beliefs. Some therapists might believe that subjecting a dysfunctional core belief to clinical scrutiny will naturally undermine it and the client will then be free of its disturbance-producing 'grip' upon him. However, as DiGiuseppe points out, challenging dysfunctional beliefs is not sufficient to change them:

> People frequently hold on to beliefs that they know are logically flawed and do not lead to accurate predictions of reality, but no alternative ideas are available to replace the flawed idea. The history of science is filled with such examples. People do not give up ideas, regardless of the evidence against the idea, unless they have an alternative idea to replace it.
>
> (1991a: 181)

Therefore, the therapist should encourage her clients to focus on how they would like to be rather than letting them linger on how they are. This focus can be initiated by asking clients something like this:

Therapist: How would you like to see yourself instead of as a 'failure'?

Client: I'm not sure.

Therapist: Let's think about it now. We don't want to spend the rest of therapy talking about you as a failure.

Client: I don't want that either. I suppose I would just like to see myself as reasonably competent.

Therapist: And what might your life look like if you were 'reasonably competent'?

Client: Well, I'd learn to take the rough with the smooth in life and not give myself a hard time when things go wrong. I'd like to be able to praise myself when I do things right. I don't know what else to say.

Therapist: That's fine. That sounds like a good start.

The therapist should not expect a client's new core belief to be fully formed and robust at the outset of schema work: the client's degree of conviction in his new belief will be gradually strengthened through the collection of evidence that supports it while his degree of conviction in his old belief will be weakened through the re-examination of evidence that used to sustain it.

Core belief work can be relatively straightforward or more difficult. In the former category, the client does have an existing positive core belief ('I'm pretty likeable') but this is difficult to gain access to currently because of his low mood following a falling-out with his best friend ('I just feel that no one likes me now. We've been friends since childhood'). Padesky (1994) suggests that producing contradictory evidence ('Let's make a list of the people you still are friends with') can quickly reactivate the client's positive belief and ameliorate his low mood within a few sessions of therapy.

In the latter category, if a positive core belief is not present to which the therapist can appeal because of the client's long-standing problems which have interfered with the development of such a belief (the client has always seen himself as 'bad'), then the first step is to identify a positive belief, even if this is difficult to do given the client's disturbed state, for 'without an explicit alternative (even if it is only initially minimally believed, and that on an intellectual rather than emotional level), the patient has nowhere to "store" information contrary to their current negative belief' (Fennell, 1997: 14).

87

USE OF A CONTINUUM

Clients' negative core beliefs are often constructed in all or nothing terms such as 'You're either a success or failure in life and I'm one of life's failures'. The use of a continuum (i.e. a scale from 0 per cent to 100 per cent) introduces shades of grey into clients' thinking thereby helping them to develop more balanced and realistic appraisals of themselves, others and the world (to arrive eventually at the mid-point on the continuum). Padesky and Greenberger suggest that 'a scale or continuum is most therapeutic when it is constructed and its data evaluated for the new schema rather than the old. A small shift that strengthens the new schema is usually more hopeful for the client than a small shift that weakens the old schema' (1995: 144).

For example, if schema change is evaluated along a continuum focusing on the old belief ('I'm worthless'), the client might declare that 'I'm only 60 per cent worthless now' and see therapy as helping him to reduce his sense of worthlessness, whereas if it is evaluated along a continuum based on his new belief ('I'm okay as a person') optimism can be engendered that his new view of himself is gaining ground ('It has increased from 15 to 20 per cent since I last saw you'). When the continuum is being constructed, the therapist should help her client to define the end-points on the continuum in extreme terms so that he can see more clearly that change is occurring (if there is not a very strong contrast between these end-points, this will limit the client's perception of how much change he is achieving). In the following example, the 0 per cent, 50 per cent and 100 per cent points on the continuum are defined by the client:

NEW CORE BELIEF: 'I'M REASONABLY COMPETENT'

0%	50%	100%
Never competent	Competent and sometimes incompetent	Always competent

The client is asked where he would currently put a cross on the continuum ('At ten per cent'). The continuum can be a regular reference point to monitor clients' progress towards the mid-point based on information and evidence collected from various sources such as positive data logs (see Point 88). A few clients may want to get to the 100 per cent point eventually but this will mean that what starts out as an adaptive belief is gradually transmuted into a maladaptive one (as it is highly unlikely the client will always be competent in every endeavour he undertakes). The continuum is designed to help clients develop a rounded (not rigid) view of themselves and their experiences, so therapists should encourage their clients to 'use qualifiers – for example, "*Sometimes* I am really smart," "*Often* I am appealing to people"' (Leahy, 2003: 246; emphases in original).

88

POSITIVE DATA LOGS

These logs help the client to collect information over the coming weeks and months to support her new adaptive belief and counteract her tendency to focus only on information that confirms her maladaptive beliefs; in other words, to correct her faulty information processing style. A major difficulty in collecting positive information is the reflex of the old core belief to discredit or discount any information that contradicts it. Padesky (1994) likens this habitual response to holding a prejudice against oneself or others (Flew states that a prejudice refers to beliefs 'which are either formed prior to proper consideration of the evidence or held in defiance of it' [1975: 29]). For example, a client's new core belief is 'I am attractive to some women' but when a woman seems interested in him at a party his old belief, 'I'm unattractive to women', discounts this: 'She's only passing the time with me until she sees someone she really does fancy.' The client becomes despondent that the old belief is the 'real truth about me and I'm deluding myself in trying to believe anything different':

Therapist: What happened with that woman who seemed interested in you?
Client: She went off to chat to someone else. The story of my life.
Therapist: Why do you think she chatted to you in the first place?
Client: [shrugs his shoulders] Nobody else to talk to.
Therapist: Were you the only person at the party then?
Client: Of course not. The room was quite crowded.
Therapist: How was she behaving towards you?
Client: She was bright and bubbly I would say.

Therapist: How did you respond?

Client: I tried to be bright and bubbly back but I was thinking 'I fancy you but I know you don't fancy me. You don't really want to talk to me'.

Therapist: What happened with those thoughts in mind?

Client: I struggled to continue the conversation. I was too much in my own head, distracted by those thoughts, and not focused on what she was saying. I felt very uncomfortable and things started getting a bit awkward and then she drifted off towards someone else.

Therapist: Is it possible that she might have stayed longer in your company if you had held up your end of the conversation?

Client: It's possible.

Therapist: Is it also possible that she was talking to you in the first place because she might have fancied you or, at least, you looked interesting to her?

Client: Yes, that's possible too. Okay, I know what you're driving at. I'm willing to concede just a little that she may have been attracted to or interested in me and I messed things up.

When clients have little or no conviction in their new adaptive beliefs, it can be very difficult for them to extract any positive information from their daily experiences; therefore, the therapist needs to be alert in every session to help her clients identify schema-supporting information, i.e. for them to be open-minded rather than closed-minded in processing information which support their new beliefs.

89

ACTING 'AS IF'

This refers to a client acting as if his new belief was true even though he may not strongly believe it at the present time. Acting in support of a new belief strengthens it, which encourages further schema-consistent behaviour which then, in turn, further strengthens the belief – and so on until it is internalized. The client is advised to pick a particular situation or arena in which to start acting 'as if' rather than attempt to promote his 'new self' straight away in many situations as he is highly likely to feel overwhelmed with the immensity of the task he has taken on. McKay and Fanning recommend that

> for your first arena, pick an area of your life in which you feel relatively safe. Don't try to tackle your most intense relationships or the responsibilities that you find most stressful. Look for a clearly defined part of your life in which you have a pretty high degree of control, with ample opportunities to put your new beliefs and rules into action.
>
> (1991: 112)

For example, a client whose new core belief was 'I can be efficient and organized' chose to clean the interior of his car as a first and safe step in acting in support of his new belief and then, over the following weeks, looked for other avoided chores to tackle in and outside his house before moving on to more challenging areas of his life such as putting his finances in order. Acting 'as if' eventually becomes 'I am': 'It sounds like magic, but you really do become what you pretend to be' (McKay and Fanning, 1991: 119). Dobson suggests that 'behavioral enactment [acting "as if"] is perhaps the single most potent technique for schema change' (2012: 91). I (MN) sometimes act 'as if' I am more confident than I really am when addressing a large audience; this helps me to keep my nervousness under control and improve my performance so that I do actually start to feel more confident during the presentation.

A major difficulty in acting 'as if' is the unfamiliarity and strangeness of the new behaviour which some clients say makes them feel like a 'phoney' and they conclude, 'This is not me'. This difficulty can lead to client discouragement to continue acting 'as if' or even to its termination. However, the therapist can reassure her clients that feeling strange or unfamiliar is a natural part of the change process and encourage them to continue by learning to tolerate these uncomfortable feelings during this transitional phase from old to new ways of behaving. As we say to our clients: 'If you ain't feeling strange, you ain't experiencing change!' Acting differently indicates newness, not phoniness. Hauck (1982) suggests that what clients regard as phoney behaviour is nothing more than breaking in a new pair of shoes.

90

HISTORICAL TEST OF THE NEW CORE BELIEF

Maladaptive core beliefs are usually formed in childhood and the client may have collected a lot of evidence over the years to support and strengthen them. However, this evidence which demonstrates the 'truth' about herself and her life is a product of the consistently negative bias generated by these beliefs. Undertaking a retrospective survey of the client's life viewed through the lens of the new core belief can be for her both productive and strange. Padesky (1994) suggests dividing the client's life into time periods (e.g. 0–2, 3–5, 6–12 years), and recommends starting the survey when the client was a baby or small child as she is unlikely to condemn herself during this period. It is important that time is spent in the present constructing and acting in support of the new core belief before going back into the past; going back with the old core belief still dominant will make the client's task harder to find supporting evidence for the new belief. In the following example, the client is examining her teenage years (13–18 years):

Therapist: Can you think of any evidence that supports your new core belief 'I am a reasonably likeable person' in this period of your life?

Client: It's hard to think of any. I was generally lonely and miserable.

Therapist: Was that because you were off school for considerable periods with all the illnesses you had?

Client: That didn't help, that's for sure.

Therapist: Did anyone from school come to see you at home when you were ill?

Client: A few girls from my class came to see me.

Therapist: Was that because they liked you or were they just doing their duty for the school, so to speak?

Client: Well, if they were doing their duty for the school they would have been polite and not stayed long. No, they were friendly towards me. We chatted and laughed for a few hours. Sometimes they stayed quite late in the evening.

Therapist: So they came more than once then? [client nods] What do you think might have happened if you had not been off school for long periods with your ill health?

Client: There's a good chance I would have had more friends. I never thought of that.

Therapist: Something else to think about too: having frequent illnesses and being off school for considerable periods led to a lot of social isolation. These were facts of your teenage years. Did you turn these facts against yourself to prove you were unlikeable?

Client : Thinking about it now, I'm sure that's what I did. Illness and isolation were not my fault. I could still be likeable even though I was not enjoying life that much at the time or had many friends.

Padesky and Greenberger state that 'it is not necessary to identify many experiences that support the new schema; even a few are meaningful to clients. Ideally, clients find one or two experiences per age period' (1995: 150).

91

CHALLENGING EACH THOUGHT IN THE DOWNWARD ARROW PROCEDURE

In Point 81 we demonstrated the downward arrow procedure to uncover a core belief. While using the downward arrow we noted it was very important for the therapist to accept each thought revealed as temporarily true, otherwise challenging each one as it appears will prevent the therapist from uncovering the core belief. However, once the core belief has been revealed, the therapist can now help the client to challenge each thought in order to modify it (Blackburn and Davidson, 1995; Burns, 1999). To return to the example in Point 81, the client is very worried about her husband's sudden willingness to stay late at work:

Thought: He might be having an affair.

Adaptive response: He might be but, on the other hand, he might be working late for perfectly legitimate reasons. Instead of torturing myself over this issue I will ask him why he has chosen now to start working late.

Thought: Well he's going to run off with the bitch.

Adaptive response: I'm running ahead of myself. I need to establish if he is having an affair and will run off with her – two separate issues. Calling her a bitch won't make me feel better and overlooks the fact that it takes two to tango. Based on what I know of my husband in the last

	ten years I very much doubt he is having an affair.
Thought:	I'll be all alone, unwanted.
Adaptive response:	I won't be all alone or unwanted. My children and friends will be there for me if he did run off – I can depend on them in times of crisis. I'm painting too gloomy a picture. I'm quite a strong person deep down so I'll be able to soldier on if he does leave me. I won't be moping around saying 'Poor me' all over the place. So when I say I'll be unwanted, I'll still want me. I'm not going to desert me even if he has.
Core belief:	That I'm unattractive, repulsive.
Adaptive response:	This is really going over the top. I may not be attractive to my husband any longer but that doesn't make me unattractive. I had my fair share of relationships before I met my husband and I've had the come-on several times while I've been married but I was never interested as I love my husband. As for being repulsive, this is absurd. I'm not thinking straight. An accurate description of myself is that I am attractive and I will regularly remind myself of that. I can pull men if I want to. If my husband has left me, then there will be new opportunities for me.

The client established that her husband's reasons for working late were indeed work-related, not because he was having an affair with a colleague, and her worries disappeared. However, she found that doing this exercise provided her with a coping strategy if her husband did leave at some future date and helped to strengthen her adaptive belief about herself.

92

'HEAD–GUT' ROLE PLAY

Clients often complain of a tension between 'head thinking' and 'gut thinking'. The former refers to a light conviction in a new adaptive core belief ('I know the new core belief is rational and sensible and will help me but …') while the latter focuses on a deep conviction in the old maladaptive core belief ('my old belief really feels like the truth about me'). 'Head–gut' role play is a procedure which encourages the client to strengthen her conviction in her new belief and weaken her conviction in her old one. This is done by the client first attempting to convince herself that her old core belief ('I'm stupid') is true by marshalling all the evidence that appears to support it and then, second, challenging this evidence point by point in order to develop more balanced and realistic interpretations of the same evidence to buttress her new core belief ('I'm a reasonably intelligent person'). Kuehlwein states that the client should challenge the evidence 'vehemently and firmly', and 'once the therapist is satisfied that the client has explored this second side fully, he checks for a reduction in belief level in the old core belief and in the accompanying distress. If it does not occur, the exercise may be repeated' (2002: 27).

It is unlikely that clients will be able to carry out this procedure without prompting from the therapist to gather all the evidence that supports her old belief (e.g. 'Don't forget that one of the reasons you believe you're stupid is because you left school with only basic qualifications'); and to ensure that her challenges to this evidence are considered and balanced (e.g. 'Do you think you are defining intelligence solely on the basis of academic qualifications and overlooking the fact that intelligence involves a wide variety of factors? For example, you're skilled at DIY, car mechanics and have never been in debt. Are these things signs of intelligence?'). At times, the therapist may need to demonstrate 'head–gut' role play before the client attempts it.

Another example of 'head–gut' role play is devil's advocate disputing (Dryden, 1995). In this technique, the client states his new core belief ('I'm generally a successful person') and his present level of conviction in it (e.g. '40 per cent'). The therapist attempts, with increasing forcefulness, to undermine the client's conviction in his new belief (e.g. 'You've had more setbacks than successes recently, so how in heaven's name can you call yourself successful?'). The client is encouraged to counter each of the therapist's arguments vigorously with a strong defence of his new belief ('My definition of a successful person includes setbacks. Learning from each setback is a sign of success') until the therapist has no arguments to present. If the client finds it difficult to deal with a particular argument of the therapist's, she will stop the exercise temporarily in order to help the client find a strong counter-argument and then resume the exercise. At the end of the exercise, the client re-rates his level of conviction in his new core belief (e.g. '60 per cent'). If the rating has gone up considerably or a little, stayed the same or even decreased (e.g. 'One of your arguments felt like a knock-out blow'), the reasons for each outcome need to be elicited and discussed.

93

LEARNING SELF-ACCEPTANCE

Clients often describe themselves in global terms (e.g. 'I'm not good enough'): 'an image of the self *as a whole person*, rather than a differentiated flexible appreciation of varying qualities or aspects of the self. By definition, it is negative or derogatory; the person is weighed in the balance and found wanting' (Fennell, 1997: 2; emphasis in original). Global ratings of the self can never capture its complexity or totality (this applies equally to positive core beliefs: calling oneself 'a genius' may be correct in your particular field, like mathematics or physics, but it does not accurately describe every aspect of your life or personality). A trait, attribute, behaviour or performance does not equal the person; when clients conclude that it does they are making the 'part equals whole' error such as 'My performance in that situation was inferior, so that makes *me* inferior'.

Self-acceptance means rating aspects of the self, but not the self on the basis of these aspects: 'My performance in that situation was inferior judged by the feedback and evaluation forms which I want to learn from in order to improve my performance, but my performance can never sum me up as a person.' It also means looking at oneself in the round by acknowledging one's positive qualities and shortcomings and attempting to change the latter if so desired; and frequently reminding oneself that human fallibility cannot be eradicated (so do not waste time trying!) but that the incidence of fallible behaviour can be reduced by learning from one's mistakes in order to make fewer of them (condemning oneself for making mistakes will add nothing of value to this learning process).

Self-acceptance greatly reduces the frequency, intensity and duration of experiencing negative emotions (e.g. shame, guilt, depression) because you stop attacking yourself which is often the cognitive core of these emotions (Neenan and Dryden, 2014). In the following dialogue, the therapist helps the client to strengthen his existing positive core belief by adding self-acceptance to it:

Therapist: You generally see yourself as what you call a 'can-do guy'.

Client: Yes, I get things done. When I put my mind to it I usually see it through but then I come up against something I can't seem to deal with and … I don't know. I just seem to get all despairing and end up seeing myself as a failure.

Therapist: How would you like to cope when you come up against something you can't seem to deal with?

Client: Well, accept that this is one nut I can't crack no matter how hard I try and not get all upset about it.

Therapist: Would you also like to accept yourself for not being able to crack this particular nut or any other uncrackable nuts that may lie in the future?

Client: That seems much more preferable than calling myself a failure and all that goes with it.

Therapist: Okay, what would you need to add to your belief 'I'm a can-do guy' in order to remind yourself of that?

Client: Hmm … Something like 'I'm a can-do guy but not always'. That seems all right, that might work.

Therapist: How might you strengthen that belief in your mind?

Client: Keep on going over it so when I do come up against the next difficulty it will be my safety net, so to speak.

The client kept a 'can-do but not always' diary to note his accomplishments and record his difficulties without despair or self-condemnation. At the post-therapy follow-up appointments (see Point 97), the client said that the addition of the 'but not always' to his existing belief had 'helped me see the value of self-acceptance and I spend much less time now dwelling on my failures or setbacks'.

Unlike the possibility with self-esteem, self-acceptance does not involve a loss of identity (Neenan and Dryden, 2002). 'Esteem' is derived from the verb 'to estimate', which means to give something or someone a rating. The concept of self-esteem suggests that a person can be rated globally (e.g. 'I'm a success because I've just been promoted and I have the respect and admiration of my colleagues'). Loss of self-esteem can lead to loss of identity if favourable conditions are reversed (the client loses her job in a company merger and has little, if any, contact with her former colleagues: 'I stare in the mirror every morning and wonder, "Who am I? Where's my life gone?"'). Self-acceptance is not based on certain criteria being met (e.g. having friends, good looks, being slim, having approval from others) in order to validate one's self-worth or identity. If self-acceptance does have an identity, it is the acknowledgement of oneself as a fallible, complex, unrateable human being – this view of oneself can remain constant whatever the circumstances in one's life. We believe that self-acceptance is one of the most important concepts that therapists can teach their clients to help them avoid rating the self which is implied by self-esteem. Self-acceptance is a project to work on across the lifespan, not just while in therapy.

94

RELAPSE REDUCTION

Instilling hope in clients that they can change is an important part of therapy; addressing the likelihood of relapse is perhaps equally as important (Feltham and Dryden, 2006). Relapse prevention (RP) originated in the treatment of substance abuse (Marlatt and Gordon, 1985) but is now applied to therapy generally. A relapse is a complete return to a previous problem state, while a lapse is a partial return to a previous problem state. By the time therapy is drawing to a close, clients will have learnt, if they did not know it already, that change is not a smooth, linear process but a series of advances and setbacks which they already have experienced in therapy. Therefore, RP promises too much – we prefer the term 'relapse reduction or management' as these terms more accurately describe the post-therapy progress of fallible human beings. Relapse reduction is a realistic strategy to pursue by pinpointing future situations (e.g. interpersonal strife, intense negative feelings, being alone) that could trigger a relapse and helping clients to develop coping plans in order to deal with these situations (these coping plans are essentially the tools and techniques they have already learnt in therapy).

Clients can imagine themselves in these situations and rehearse their coping strategies (these exercises can be carried out as if they were happening in the present rather than the future). For example, a client who said that he would be tempted to start drinking again after a row with his partner because he would have difficulty tolerating his angry feelings, wrote his alternative thoughts and behaviours on a card: 'Call a friend from AA [Alcoholics Anonymous] to talk things through'; 'Go to a quiet part of the house to calm down'; 'Listen to relaxing music'; 'Go to the gym'; 'Forcefully remind myself that I don't need alcohol to help me through a bad situation. I am determined to face it with a clear head'; 'When I've calmed down, talk to my partner without name-calling, self-condemnation or shouting and apologize for any unpleasant behaviour I may have engaged in.'

Clients can learn that a lapse (e.g. having a drink, not keeping to a diet) does not automatically lead to a relapse – no slippery slope inevitability – if they are prepared to deal with it as soon as it has occurred by accepting that lapses are part of progress, by drawing out the lessons that can be learnt from the slip to improve coping strategies in vulnerable situations (e.g. changes undertaken are not yet complete, relapse is a product of choice even if the choice is not always apparent or conscious [Ellis *et al.*, 1988]); avoiding all-or-nothing thinking (e.g. 'Once a drunk, always a drunk'; 'As I've wrecked my diet, there's no point keeping to it') as this usually turns a lapse into a relapse (Beck *et al.*, 1993). Lapses/relapses are incidents in the change process, not its whole story which some discouraged clients can come to believe.

Relapse management helps clients to understand that slips are opportunities for learning rather than signs of personal inadequacy, and after a slip they can put themselves 'back on track' (Marlatt and Gordon, 1985). Leahy (2003) suggests reframing a relapse as a learning or natural experiment, i.e. what happens when the client does not follow the guidelines for maintaining progress after therapy has ended.

95

TERMINATION

The end of therapy is often discussed at its outset: by working with the therapist, the client will learn a range of self-help skills to implement both in and between sessions in order to become his own problem-solver and will terminate therapy in that capacity. As the client gains both confidence and competence in managing his difficulties, sessions are tapered off (e.g. from weekly to fortnightly to monthly) with the therapist now reconceptualizing her role as the client's coach or consultant (the client has largely taken over her original role). It can be useful to have a 'countdown' approach to termination by reminding the client (and the therapist) in each session of how many sessions are left of the agreed treatment programme in order to gain maximum therapeutic benefit from them. A rush to termination or an arbitrary decision on the therapist's part ('We'll make this session the last one') can undo the benefits of therapy:

> For this reason, it is important that the process of completion of therapy be handled as effectively and as smoothly as possible. When the conclusion of therapy is handled well, the patient is more likely to consolidate gains and to generalize strategies for handling future problems.
>
> (Beck *et al.*, 1979: 317)

The client can be asked to summarize his gains from therapy, in particular those ideas and techniques he found especially valuable; these gains can be written down on a card and kept in the client's wallet for easy access. For example, the client says that 'putting my thinking under the spotlight really showed me how much of an all-or-nothing thinker I really was'. Two ideas he will particularly hold on to are: (1) thoughts are usually hypotheses, not facts, and 'therefore I can change them by examining them'; and (2) he can choose how he reacts to situations: 'Before CBT, I believed that situations made me angry, but now I realize I have more options to choose from in deciding how I want to react.' A technique he found very helpful was progressive muscle relaxation (systematically tensing and relaxing the major muscle groups of the body while maintaining a slow breathing rate) 'as I can't be angry and relaxed at the same time and I'd rather be relaxed'. An action plan was developed to deal with future problematic situations which might trigger prolonged angry outbursts (see Point 94 on relapse reduction).

Clients often have concerns about termination which the therapist needs to address. Some of these concerns are:

- 'I won't be able to cope on my own.' The client has already been coping on her own by carrying out homework assignments; also, she will still be able to hear the voice of the therapist providing encouragement and support, so she will not be psychologically on her own and therefore can engage in an imaginal consultation with the therapist when struggling to cope in times of difficulty. The client can view her prediction as in need of empirical testing (like all her other predictions in therapy) by striking out alone.
- 'Not all my problems have been sorted out.' Therapy is not intended to sort out all the client's problems, just some of them. The client's self-help skills can be applied to these other problems post-therapy; to have resolved all the client's problems before he leaves therapy undermines the idea of becoming a self-therapist and risks the client becoming dependent upon the therapist to do all his problem-solving for him.
- 'I'm not cured yet.' Again, therapy is never intended to 'cure' the client but to reduce the frequency, intensity and duration of his problems; in other words, to manage them more effectively. Self-management becomes more effective through the client applying his CBT skills in problematic situations and learning from his experiences.

- 'I haven't told you what the real problem is.' This statement can give the impression that therapy up to this point has been a prelude to the 'real stuff' (e.g. sexual abuse) being explored, but now it is too late as therapy has come to an end. The therapist can explore briefly why the client has revealed this issue at the last minute and choose whether or not to extend counselling; decide to keep to the agreed problem list, not add to it; suggest that the client can contact him at a later date for another course of counselling focusing on the 'real stuff'; or refer the client to another therapist. The therapist should not feel trapped or blackmailed into automatically extending therapy.

- 'I'm getting all anxious again, so it can't be time for me to go.' As termination nears, some clients feel understandably apprehensive about going it alone and see themselves 'falling apart' post-therapy. These fears trigger a reactivation of their presenting symptoms which gives the impression to these clients that they are actually getting worse, not better. They can be reminded that feelings are not facts (e.g. 'Just because I feel that I will relapse as soon as therapy ends does not mean that I will'); that this is a common experience as termination approaches; that they have made considerable progress as self-therapists despite their present apprehension; and that what happens after therapy is not yet 'written' – their self-therapy diaries could tell of coping rather than of catastrophe.

While clients are usually appreciative of the therapist's efforts ('I couldn't have done it without your help'), it is important for the therapist to resist the temptation of taking too much credit for the client's success ('Well, now you come to mention it ...') and place the major credit where it belongs – with the client. Wills and Sanders (1997) suggest pointing out to clients that they have been working on their problems for 24 hours a day, seven days a week while the therapist has only put in a session time of, for example, eight, ten or twelve hours. Finally, termination should not be viewed by the therapist as an inevitably sad or wrenching experience for clients: some clients, while pleased with their progress, will want a business-like end to therapy.

MAINTAINING GAINS
FROM THERAPY

Achieving one's goals is not the same process as maintaining them (e.g. getting fit, then staying fit; losing weight, then keeping to the new weight). Some clients might believe that once therapy is terminated their therapeutic gains will 'magically' stay intact without any further input from them, that they deserve a prolonged rest after all their hard work in therapy, or that therapy was a discrete, crisis-driven episode that they now can thankfully put behind them (Neenan and Dryden, 2011). In our experience, clients can quickly fall back into old self-defeating patterns of thinking and behaving by taking their 'eye off the ball' – i.e. not practising consistently their hard-won CBT skills – so a maintenance outlook needs to be developed by them to reduce the chances of such an outcome occurring.

To initiate a discussion on this issue, the therapist can ask: 'How will you keep your progress going after therapy ends?' or 'Does ten sessions of therapy provide you with a lifelong guarantee that you will never slip back?' In essence, a maintenance outlook, idiosyncratically tailored, is required to keep and strengthen the client's gains from therapy. For example, one client's maintenance message was 'use them [CBT skills] or lose them' while another client's was 'check regularly my cognitive circuits' (he worked as an electrician). Beck (2011) suggests that clients can schedule self-therapy sessions, modelled on CBT sessions, where they set an agenda which would include designing and reviewing homework tasks, assessing progress, dealing with current difficulties and troubleshooting future ones. Clients can put the dates for self-therapy sessions in their diary (though we doubt many clients will be interested in undertaking these sessions).

Clients can be alert for warning signs that they might be heading for a setback and have a prepared action plan to hand (family and friends can also be involved in looking out for warning signs). Here are some examples.

- A client feels hot and uncomfortable in a supermarket queue and has the urge to 'run outside' to escape an imagined catastrophe. However, the client vigorously reminds himself that his panicky symptoms are harmless, not dangerous, based on the experiments he conducted in therapy: 'My panicky feelings will pass quickly like they've always done and I'll be fine as always, so keep calm.' He also remembers the five-minute rule he learnt in therapy:

  > If you stop scaring yourself with anxious thoughts, panic can't last more than five minutes. It's a medical reality. Because adrenaline from the fight-or-flight reaction is metabolized in five minutes or less, panic will end if new anxious thoughts don't cause the release of more adrenaline.
  >
  > (McKay *et al.*, 2011: 89)

  (Controlling his thoughts controlled his panic; the client stayed in the queue and his symptoms subsided.)
- A wife points out to her husband that 'you're doing it again, darling', i.e. brooding on mistakes he made at work. Past mistakes resulted in low mood and self-condemnation. Now, his wife's 'nudge' encourages him to go over a valuable lesson from therapy: 'Mistakes are inevitable; getting upset over them is not.' With this thought in mind, he makes a few notes on how he can rectify and learn from his mistakes.
- A client starts to feel 'clingy' again in her relationship as old fears of being unloveable and abandoned resurface. In order to strengthen her belief that she does not need love in order to be happy or to prove her worth, she spends some time alone. This reaffirms her ability to enjoy her own company. As the client tells her partner: 'When the clinginess goes, we have a much better time.'

Another way of maintaining and strengthening therapeutic gains is for the client to teach others some of the CBT skills he learnt in therapy, e.g. explaining to a friend that she should consider all the factors that contributed to the end of her marriage instead of blaming herself for the break up: 'I learnt in therapy to look at the whole picture, not just my part in it' (see Point 55 on reattribution). Through teaching others, the client continues to deepen his understanding of these valuable problem-solving methods. However, it is important that the client does not present himself to others as a 'know-all' or paragon of problem-solving wisdom as this is likely to alienate rather than encourage them to listen and learn. Clients can also use their CBT skills in other problem areas of their life they may have been avoiding tackling or which have recently arisen – e.g., respectively, standing up to an overbearing work colleague or firmly requesting new neighbours to turn down their loud music.

CBT skills are not only used for overcoming present and future problems but also in the service of ambition and realizing important life goals (Neenan and Dryden, 2014). For example, a client who entered therapy to tackle a bout of depression and worry decided, on recovery, that he wanted to fulfil his long-standing desire to be self-employed. He developed an action plan to help him achieve this goal. In follow-up appointments (see Point 97) his recovery was monitored, as was to be expected, but the therapist also spent some time discussing the client's progress towards becoming self-employed and how he was dealing with roadblocks he encountered along the way.

97

FOLLOW-UP

How will the therapist know whether or not her clients are maintaining their therapeutic gains or determine the effectiveness of her treatment approach if she never sees them again once therapy ends? Follow-up appointments such as in three, six and twelve months' time can be offered to clients in order to monitor their progress as self-therapists – how firmly have they consolidated their gains from therapy? The therapist should allow sufficient time to elapse before arranging a follow-up in order to determine the extent of the client's progress without the therapist's support (Cormier and Cormier, 1985). For example, if the client has spent ten sessions in therapy over a period of three months, then the first follow-up can be scheduled in three months' time. It should be made clear to clients that follow-up sessions are not therapy sessions. Follow-up also offers clients a longer-term perspective from which to reflect on their experiences of therapy and what they have learnt from it. A client I (MN) saw at a 12-month follow-up appointment said that it was only now that she was beginning to really appreciate and benefit from what she had learnt in therapy about replacing self-esteem with self-acceptance (see Point 93 for a discussion of these two concepts). Follow-up provides useful information for the therapist in reviewing her work with clients and finding out what they found helpful and unhelpful about it (Feltham and Dryden, 2006).

Some clients feel safer about terminating therapy as their therapeutic progress is still being 'kept an eye on' by the therapist, though follow-ups are not meant to keep therapy going under the guise of monitoring progress. Sometimes clients find that difficulties which have emerged post-therapy are, after a period of personal struggle with them, too difficult to deal with on their own; if this is the case, then they can contact the therapist to arrange an appointment ahead of the official follow-up. Such a contingency arrangement is usually agreed in the final session of formal therapy. If the client has deteriorated since the end of therapy, the reasons for this should be elicited (e.g. the client has experienced a number of setbacks in his life which he describes as 'doing my head in and my CBT skills weren't much help'). He can be offered a brief top-up or revision period of therapy – not another full course of CBT as this may convey to the client that all his previously hard-won progress was actually an illusion (e.g. 'I obviously did not understand anything about CBT the first time around'). What the client did not fully understand was the crucial importance of developing a post-therapy maintenance of gains outlook (see Point 96) and therapy became a distant memory for him several days after it ended.

98

PRACTISING WHAT YOU PREACH

Do cognitive behavioural therapists practise CBT on themselves when they encounter difficulties, both inside and outside therapy? Not always as some subscribe to the myth of the untroubled therapist (Adams, 2014). Our experience of training and supervising therapists shows us that some individuals believe that CBT is something they do to 'them' (i.e. clients) and is not performed on themselves – cognitive behavioural mechanics 'fixing' others' problems but not their own. This attitude is unfortunate as it can lead these therapists to practise CBT without a genuine conviction in it, not appreciate the difficulties their clients have in implementing CBT skills in their everyday lives (and likely to call them 'resistant' when progress is stalled), and do what is necessary to be seen as a competent practitioner (such as further training, attending workshops, and having regular supervision) but lack the experiential element of using it on themselves. Furthermore, if some of these therapists do eventually go for personal therapy they are likely to choose a different approach such as psychodynamic therapy: 'I know all about CBT. I do it every day. I want to try something new and different for myself.' We would make three observations about this response.

1 It is a rash person who claims to 'know all about CBT'. We doubt that Aaron Beck, the founder of cognitive therapy, would make this claim as he has outlined some areas in CBT for future research (Beck and Dozois, 2011). In our experience, those who claim to know all about CBT still have not grasped the breadth and depth of this approach and therefore believe that their problems cannot be contained within the model. And a few therapists,

regrettably, subscribe to misrepresentations of CBT, e.g. 'Well, let's face it, CBT is essentially replacing negative thinking with positive thinking, isn't it?' (see Point 14) – maybe that is how they have been practising it over the years! With this viewpoint, the therapist would be practising CBT on autopilot and possibly not much more enlightened about this approach at the end of his career than he was at the beginning of it.

2   Trying 'something new and different for myself' would be receiving CBT as a client instead of delivering it as a therapist. Padesky points out that a 'final process [after training and supervision] that enhances the competency of cognitive therapists is participating in cognitive therapy as a client. To fully understand the process of the therapy, there is no substitute for using cognitive therapy methods on oneself' (1996: 288). Some therapists find another approach a better substitute.

3   Practising CBT but entering a non-CBT approach for personal therapy suggests a schism between head and heart: the head responds to the empirically validated, active-directive, time-limited, structured approach of CBT for dealing with a heavy caseload, but the heart yearns for untrammelled exploration and discussion – divested of forms, inventories, agendas, session targets, goals and homework 'where I can really be myself and wander where I want when I want' as some therapists have said to us. While these therapists may be technically proficient in their practice of CBT, they are presenting an inauthentic self to their clients because if asked by them if they use CBT on themselves, the answer would have to be an emphatic 'No!' By examining and restructuring their own dysfunctional cognitions, therapists remain congruent with what they say in public and do in private and thereby act authentically with their clients.

If the therapist does opt for CBT it is probably best not to choose a colleague for the following reasons: this 'chumminess' might prevent frank disclosure from the client ('Do I really want her to know *that* about me?');

complacency may occur as two CBT 'experts' discuss the client's case as if it was peer supervision and only tangentially connected to the client's concerns; tension might develop as the client puts the therapist 'through her paces' to see how competent she actually is and the therapist seeks to impress her colleague with her skills; and therapy may prove unproductive which results in a 'strained' post-therapy relationship which might also be felt in the department.

In our experience, some CBT therapists who do enter CBT therapy downplay the effectiveness of the very same procedures they have used successfully with their own clients in order to prove to the therapist that their problems are too complex for CBT to handle; rattle off CBT terminology to try and impress the therapist without displaying any conviction in what they are saying; or are simply baffled as to how to apply CBT to themselves.

RESISTANCE

The central paradox of psychotherapy might be defined as those clients who seek help to overcome their psychological difficulties, then apparently resist the attempts of the therapist to help them achieve this goal. The concept of resistance in therapy derives from the psychodynamic literature involving a client's opposition to the therapist's attempts to make her unconscious wishes and impulses conscious. A CBT-oriented view of resistance would focus on therapy-interfering beliefs and behaviours whether exhibited by clients and/or therapists. Leahy defines client resistance in CBT as 'anything in the patient's behavior, thinking, affective [emotional] response, and interpersonal style that interferes with the ability of that patient to utilize the treatment and to acquire the ability to handle problems outside of therapy and after therapy has been terminated' (2001: 11). These 'interferences' may include homework non-compliance, endless 'yes, but ...' statements, not adhering to the agreed session agenda, always being late for therapy or missing appointments frequently, not taking responsibility for change, focusing on issues that are not clinically relevant, being overly compliant with everything the therapist suggests, and jumping from problem to problem before any productive changes have occurred with the previous one – these and other therapy-interfering activities will militate against the client becoming his own therapist which is the ultimate goal of CBT. Kwee and Lazarus state that 'resistance is bound to occur whenever one tries to exert influence on somebody else. Otherwise therapy would be a simple job, for it would then be sufficient merely to tell the client what to do' (1986: 333).

A client's resistance to change may seem inexplicable or baffling to the therapist, but it makes sense *to the client* if the therapist has the wit to probe for the reasons behind this apparently recalcitrant behaviour. For example, a client who was diagnosed with post-traumatic stress disorder (PTSD) following a street mugging was avoiding more and more situations as she experienced a growing sense of unease and danger in her life. The therapist in supervision with me (MN) was complaining about her homework non-compliance (entering and staying in avoided situations as part of the treatment plan). Listening to a digital voice recording (DVR) of the client session, I thought that the therapist was trying to move the client too quickly through the treatment plan in order to make progress which would then confirm his CBT competence (the need to keep confirming one's clinical competence is a perennial theme in supervision), and 'the treatment protocol says exposure is important so that's what I'm doing'. I suggested to him that therapy had probably become another threatening situation for her to avoid because of his eagerness for her to start situational exposure. This indeed turned out to be the case and once the therapist guaranteed that the pace of therapy would be under her control, not his, she returned to therapy and progress in situational exposure was later made. If only the therapist had spoken directly to the client about these issues a few months earlier!

Difficulties brought to therapy by some clients include: trusting the therapist, being in two minds about changing the status quo in their lives, expending variable effort to execute homework tasks accompanied by 'Is it worth it?' ruminations, trying to understand their problems through the CBT lens which is so different from their own deeply entrenched world views, feeling strange (e.g. 'I'm not me anymore. I'm not sure I like it') as they start to think and act in unfamiliar ways. None of these difficulties have to be seen as resistance but, instead, as self-protective processes which guide clients to assess carefully each step in therapy to determine whether to leave or continue with it.

With regard to the first difficulty brought by some clients, a therapist might complain that the client 'doesn't really trust me and I'm not getting the full picture of her problems; she's resistant about opening up'. If the therapist had paid close attention to the client's case conceptualization which he developed with her, then he would see that one of her key underlying assumptions is: 'If I put my trust in people, then they will let me down very badly.' Again, the client's logic makes perfect sense in being reluctant to trust this stranger, otherwise known as the therapist who has to gain her trust over time. However, even if clients' reasons for their resistance are made manifest and addressed, it does not automatically follow that making progress might now be a bit easier or they will be more likely to stay in therapy because clients are still engaged in an internal struggle 'that leads many [of them] to resist changing themselves outside and inside of therapy' (Ellis, 2002: 46). Leahy suggests that if the therapist can adopt an attitude of curiosity towards clients' resistance and see it as part of the 'collaborative experience of therapy' instead of personalizing it (e.g. 'Why is this client behaving like this towards me when I'm trying to help him'), then 'by getting into their shoes, we can help them find the pathway out [of their difficulties]' (2001: 287).

Therapist resistance impedes clients' progress. When some therapists label their clients as 'resistant' they might be putting the label on the wrong person. Lazarus and Fay (1982) state that resistance is the therapist's rationalization to explain his treatment failures. Therapist resistance in CBT might include: setting the agenda and homework tasks unilaterally instead of collaboratively; seeking to confirm his hypotheses about clients' problems rather than conducting therapy in a spirit of open-minded inquiry; setting ambitious goals for clients in order to demonstrate his great abilities; applying treatment protocols rigidly; lecturing too much instead of asking questions and not listening and responding to clients' concerns; blaming the client for every difficulty encountered; and treating clients as if their main purpose in therapy is to appreciate the therapist's 'wisdom'.

Tackling these issues can start with the therapist having regular supervision with a competent supervisor which includes listening to lots of DVRs of his therapy sessions, and reading to increase his understanding of resistance – his own and his clients' (e.g. Beck, 2005; Ellis, 2002). Harder to develop is self-awareness that alerts the therapist in the first place to his own counter-therapeutic behaviour in therapy and, when noticed, then depends on his reluctance or determination to address it. Like any other therapist quality, self-awareness is in short supply for some therapists.

Sometimes client and therapist join together to impede progress as when they get on 'too well' and thereby distract themselves from the more mundane tasks of therapy such as tackling the client's psychological difficulties. In such cases, the paradox is that if the client improves, the social side of therapy is threatened. As a result, collusion may occur between the therapist and client to avoid making therapy as effective as possible. With such therapists, we instruct them in supervision to reorient therapy to its primary purpose of problem-solving by probing for emotionally upsetting cognitions and then both therapist and client embrace the 'cognitive strain' of finding adaptive responses to them. The outcome of this strategy is usually a sharp decline in the 'fun' side of therapy.

THIRD WAVE CBT

This refers to newer versions of CBT. According to Mansell and Taylor (2012), the first wave was the separate development of behaviour therapy and cognitive therapy in the 1950s and 1960s; the second occurred in the 1980s with the merging of cognitive and behavioural approaches (CBT). The third wave emerged in the 1990s with such approaches as Acceptance and Commitment Therapy (ACT; Hayes *et al.*, 2011), Mindfulness-Based Cognitive Therapy (MBCT; Segal *et al.*, 2013) and Dialectical Behaviour Therapy (DBT; Linehan, 1993). Third wave therapies have some differences with each other but 'arguably share an emphasis on a "mindful state of awareness"' (Mansell and Taylor, 2012: 8). Where traditional CBT examines cognitive content (thoughts and beliefs) with a view to changing it, mindfulness techniques teach clients to observe their thoughts, feelings and physical sensations in the present moment without judging them or attempting to change them, no matter how intense they are. Craske (2010) summarizes third wave approaches as function over content, i.e. noticing the adverse impact that negative thinking has on emotion but disengaging from attempts to examine or dispute thoughts (content) and, instead, learning to accept our inner experiences as a way of weakening the effects of this impact.

Mindfulness teaches clients to change their relationship to these thoughts, not challenge them. Upsetting thoughts can appear stronger than they actually are because we keep arguing or pleading with them, obsessing about or trying to suppress or control them, relaxing them away or exhorting ourselves to think positive – often to no avail and we become prisoners of our negative thinking.

235

Clients are not expected to sit there all day observing their thoughts (just as CBT clients are not expected to challenge their thoughts all the time), but to engage in valued activities while accepting the thoughts and feelings are still with them; these activities are not to be used as a form of avoidance or distraction from these thoughts and feelings. For example, a depressed client might decide to go for a walk to get some fresh air and try to brighten his mood but thinks 'I'll never get any better. I'm pathetic for being like this'. The client has engaged with his thoughts and started evaluating himself again, so what does he do now?

> You can start with simply observing that you have a negative thought. It's there for this moment. Rather than try to get rid of this thought – or get angry at it – you might say, "Here you are again." You can welcome the thought. You can ask the thought to come along for a walk ... As you walk along, with the negative thought chattering away and criticizing you, you can decide to accept that it is there ... you are walking along in the present moment, observing and accepting the reality in front of you.
>
> (Leahy, 2010: 75)

It might seem that traditional CBT and third wave approaches are incompatible and to mix the two would be conceptually confusing to both client and therapist (are we supposed to examine thoughts or just observe them?). We agree that it takes a skilful CBT therapist to combine the two but she could say something like this:

> There are different ways of dealing with our upsetting thoughts. The traditional approach in CBT is to step back from these thoughts in order to examine them more objectively and find helpful responses to them. A new approach in CBT called mindfulness also requires us to step back from our thoughts but not to do anything with them. Allow them to be there, just observe them in the present moment without judgement. Both approaches lead to a decrease in the intensity of your unpleasant feelings. So if you are not making any headway in trying to change hot thoughts through the examination process, we can shift to a do nothing strategy and you can watch

these thoughts wither on the vine through neglect, so to speak. How does that sound to you?

The term 'third wave' sometimes gave the impression that traditional CBT had become passé (i.e. examining thoughts was unproductive and old hat), but in recent years the 'term is falling out of favor and there appears to be a clearer understanding that the [newer versions of CBT] simply represent a greater, and in some cases, a new focus on certain psychological processes, treatment goals, and scientific methods' (Twohig *et al.*, 2013: 227). These authors emphasize that all approaches within the CBT field continue to develop and change. Clark and Beck (2010) see these newer versions as expanding the clinical armamentarium (procedures and techniques) of CBT.

APPENDIX 1

INITIAL CASE CONCEPTUALIZATION OF A CLIENT WITH SOCIAL PHOBIA*

Predisposing factors forming client's cognitive vulnerability to future situations where his nervousness might be evident and he wants to conceal it

Earlier experiences
Remembers fear of being in the spotlight at school as this led to physical punishment by the teachers when he got things wrong: 'I stood there crying; it was so humiliating.'
Worried at college that he might make a fool of himself by appearing weak or nervous and be ostracized for it.
Tacit message: 'Don't show nervousness to others.'

Core beliefs and underlying assumptions
'I'm weak' [core belief]
'If I keep myself under control, then I'll be seen as competent and strong' (positive assumption)
'If I show uncertainty or nervousness, then I'll be ridiculed and rejected' [negative assumption]

Strategies to avoid activating core belief
Project image of strength and resilience
Work hard to get ahead in life
Attempt to remove any imperfections in his character

Precipitating event
Being appointed as chairman of an important committee, but feeling very apprehensive about it in case he shows nervousness while chairing the meetings

Core belief and negative assumption activated
He will be exposed as weak for showing the nervousness which will lead to ridicule and rejection by the committee members

Situation
Waiting to sign the minutes of the last meeting [being in the spotlight reminds him of his schooldays]

Factors maintaining client's problems	Negative automatic thoughts (NATs) 'My hand will shake uncontrollably' 'I'll be seen as nervous and out of control' 'My credibility will be destroyed' 'They won't want me as chairman'

↗	↕	↕	↘
Self-consciousness/ mind-reading	*Safety behaviours*	*Physical symptoms*	*Emotions*
'They can see how nervous I am'	Keeps tight control of himself Has pen ready Rushes signature	Heart racing Mind spinning Tightness in chest Dry mouth Trembling	Near panic

Note: * Social Phobia 'is a marked and persistent fear of one or more social or performance situations in which the person is exposed to unfamiliar people or to possible scrutiny by others. The individual fears that he or she will act in a way (or show anxiety symptoms) that will be humiliating or embarrassing' (DSM-IV-TR, American Psychiatric Association, 2000).

APPENDIX 2

DAILY THOUGHT RECORD (DTR) OF CLIENT WITH SOCIAL PHOBIA

Situation	Negative automatic thoughts	Emotions	Alternative and balanced thoughts	How do you feel now?
Describe clearly and concisely	Rate believability of thoughts (0–100%)	Rate intensity of emotions (0–100%)	Rate believability of alternative thoughts (0–100%)	Re-rate intensity of emotions (0–100%)
Waiting for the minutes of the last meeting to be passed to me for signing	My hand will shake uncontrollably (90%) I'll be seen as nervous and out of control (90%) My credibility will be destroyed (95%) They won't want me as chairman (90%)	Anxiety (90%)	It has shaken in the past but never uncontrollably (70%) I'm mind-reading again. If I want to know how they really see me, then I'll ask them (70%) It will take something far more serious than my hand shaking for my credibility to be destroyed (75%) They voted me chairman and, as far as I know, they still want me (75%)	Anxiety (40%)

APPENDIX 3

HOMEWORK ASSIGNMENT FORM FOR CLIENT WITH SOCIAL PHOBIA

1 **What is the assignment ? (State when , where and how often the assignment is to be carried out)**

This Friday evening at the meeting I will wait patiently for the minutes to be passed to me by the secretary, gently pick up my pen, glance at each page of the minutes, and then slowly write my signature. These things are done in order for me to linger in the spotlight.

2 **What is the purpose of the assignment ? (This should follow on from the work done in the session and be linked to the client's goal)**

To test my catastrophic prediction that my hand will shake uncontrollably if I do the above things rather than engage in my usual behaviour of snatching the minutes from the secretary, having my pen ready to write my signature as quickly as possible to get myself out of the spotlight. In other words, I'm going to drop my safety behaviours.

3 **Troubleshooting obstacles to homework completion**

Potential obstacle: I'll get so anxious about things going hideously wrong if I drop my safety behaviours that I'll avoid doing the assignment.

Response: I'm going to do this assignment come hell or high water. I've had enough of living with this blasted fear!

4   **Contingency planning if assignment proves too difficult to complete**

Do what I can. Note down my thoughts and feelings that blocked me from carrying out the assignment. Remind myself that these assignments are all about learning more about my problem and how to overcome it; they are definitely not about success or failure in terms of the assignment or myself.

REFERENCES

Adams, M. (2014) *The Myth of the Untroubled Therapist: Private Life, Professional Practice*. Hove: Routledge.

Altrows, I. F. (2002) 'Rational emotive and cognitive behavior therapy with adult male offenders', *Journal of Rational–Emotive and Cognitive-Behavior Therapy*, 20 (3/4): 201–222.

American Psychiatric Association (2000) *Diagnostic and Statistical Manual of Mental Disorders*, 4th edn., text revision. Washington, DC: American Psychiatric Association.

American Psychiatric Association (2013) *Diagnostic and Statistical Manual of Mental Disorders*, 5th edn. Washington, DC: American Psychiatric Association.

Barlow, D. H. and Cerny, J. A. (1988) *Psychological Treatment of Panic*. New York: Guilford.

Barlow, D. H. and Craske, M. G. (1989) *Mastery of your Anxiety and Panic*. Albany, NY: Graywind Publications.

Beck, A. T. (1976) *Cognitive Therapy and the Emotional Disorders*. New York: New American Library.

Beck, A. T. (1987) 'Cognitive models of depression', *Journal of Cognitive Psychotherapy*, 1 (1): 5–37.

Beck, A. T. (1988) *Love is Never Enough*. New York: Harper & Row.

Beck, A. T. and Dozois, D. J. A. (2011) 'Cognitive therapy: current status and future directions', *The Annual Review of Medicine*, 62: 397–409 (kindle edition).

Beck, A. T., Emery, G. and Greenberg, R. L. (1985) *Anxiety Disorders and Phobias: A Cognitive Perspective*. New York: Basic Books.

Beck, A. T., Steer, R. A. and Brown, G. K. (1996) *Beck Depression Inventory*, 2nd edn. San Antonio, TX: The Psychological Corporation.

Beck, A. T., Epstein, N., Brown, G. and Steer, R. A. (1988) 'An inventory for measuring clinical anxiety: psychometric properties', *Journal of Consulting and Clinical Psychology*, 56: 893–897.

Beck, A. T., Freeman, A., Davis, D. D. and Associates (2004) *Cognitive Therapy of Personality Disorders*, 2nd edn. New York: Guilford.

Beck, A. T., Rush, A. J., Shaw, B. F. and Emery, G. (1979) *Cognitive Therapy of Depression*. New York: Guilford.

Beck, A. T., Wright, F. D., Newman, C. F. and Liese, B. S. (1993) *Cognitive Therapy of Substance Abuse*. New York: Guilford.

Beck, J. S. (2005) *Cognitive Therapy for Challenging Problems*. New York: Guilford.

Beck, J. S. (2011) *Cognitive Behavior Therapy: Basics and Beyond*, 2nd edn. New York: Guilford.

Bennett-Levy, J., Butler, G., Fennell, M., Hackmann, A., Mueller, M. and Westbrook, D. (eds.) (2004) *Oxford Guide to Behavioural Experiments in Cognitive Therapy*. Oxford: Oxford University Press.

Blackburn, I. M. and Davidson, K. (1995) *Cognitive Therapy for Depression and Anxiety* (amended). Oxford: Blackwell Scientific Publications.

Blackburn, I. M. and Twaddle, V. (1996) *Cognitive Therapy in Action*. London: Souvenir Press.

Burns, D. D. (1989) *The Feeling Good Handbook*. New York: William Morrow.

Burns, D. D. (1999) *Feeling Good: The New Mood Therapy*, 2nd edn. New York: Avon.

Butler, G., Fennell, M. and Hackmann, A. (2008) *Cognitive-Behavioral Therapy for Anxiety Disorders*. Guilford: New York.

Clark, D. A. (1995) 'Perceived limitations of standard cognitive therapy: a consideration of efforts to revise Beck's theory and therapy', *Journal of Cognitive Psychotherapy*, 9 (3): 153–172.

Clark, D. A. and Beck, A. T. (2010) *Cognitive Therapy of Anxiety Disorders*. New York: Guilford.

Clark, D. A. and Beck, A. T. (2012) *The Anxiety and Worry Workbook: The Cognitive Behavioral Solution.* New York: Guilford.

Clark, D. A. and Steer, R. A. (1996) 'Empirical status of the cognitive model of anxiety and depression', in P. M. Salkovskis (ed.), *Frontiers of Cognitive Therapy*. New York: Guilford.

Clark, D. M. (1989) 'Anxiety states: panic and generalized anxiety', in K. Hawton, P. M. Salkovskis, J. Kirk and D. M. Clark (eds), *Cognitive Behaviour Therapy for Psychiatric Problems: A Practical Guide*. Oxford: Oxford University Press.

Clark, D. M. (1996) 'Panic disorder: from theory to therapy', in P. M. Salkovskis (ed.), *Frontiers of Cognitive Therapy*. New York: Guilford.

Cooper, M., Todd, G. and Wells, A. (2000) *Bulimia Nervosa: A Cognitive Therapy Programme for Clients.* London: Jessica Kingsley Publishers.

Cormier, W. H. and Cormier, L. S. (1985) *Interviewing Strategies for Helpers: Fundamental Skills and Cognitive Behavioral Interventions*, 2nd edn. Monterey, CA: Brooks/Cole.

Craske, M. G. (2010) *Cognitive-Behavioral Therapy*. Washington, DC: American Psychological Association.

Dattilio, F. M. and Freeman, A. (1992) 'Introduction to cognitive therapy', in A. Freeman and F. M. Dattilio (eds), *Comprehensive Casebook of Cognitive Therapy*. New York: Plenum.

Dattilio, F. M. and Padesky, C. A. (1990) *Cognitive Therapy with Couples.* Sarasota, FL: Professional Resource Exchange.

Davidson, K. (2008) *Cognitive Therapy for Personality Disorders,* 2nd edn. Hove: Routledge.

DiGiuseppe, R. (1991a) 'Comprehensive cognitive disputing in RET', in M. E. Bernard (ed.), *Using Rational–Emotive Therapy Effectively: A Practitioner's Guide*. New York: Plenum.

DiGiuseppe, R. (1991b) 'A rational–emotive model of assessment', in M. E. Bernard (ed.), *Using Rational–Emotive Therapy Effectively: A Practitioner's Guide.* New York: Plenum.

Dobson, D. and Dobson, K. S. (2009) *Evidence-Based Practice of Cognitive-Behavioral Therapy*. New York: Guilford.

Dobson, K. (2012) *Cognitive Therapy*. Washington, DC: American Psychological Association.

Dryden, W. (1995) *Brief Rational Emotive Behaviour Therapy*. Chichester: Wiley.

Edelman, S. (2006) *Change Your Thinking*. London: Vermilion.

Ellis, A. (2002) *Overcoming Resistance: A Rational Emotive Behavior Therapy Integrated Approach*, 2nd edn. New York: Springer.

Ellis, A., McInerney, J. F., DiGiuseppe, R. and Yeager, R. J. (1988) *Rational–Emotive Therapy with Alcoholics and Substance Abusers*. New York: Pergamon.

Espie, C. A. (2006) *Overcoming Insomnia and Sleep Problems*. London: Robinson.

Fairburn, C. G. (2008) *Cognitive Behavior Therapy and Eating Disorders*. New York: Guilford.

Feltham, C. and Dryden, W. (2006) *Brief Counselling: A Practical Integrative Approach*, 2nd edn. Maidenhead: Open University Press.

Fennell, M. J. V. (1989) 'Depression', in K. Hawton, P. M. Salkovskis, J. Kirk and D. M. Clark (eds), *Cognitive Behaviour Therapy for Psychiatric Problems: A Practical Guide*. Oxford: Oxford University Press.

Fennell, M. J. V. (1997) 'Low self-esteem: a cognitive perspective', *Behavioural and Cognitive Psychotherapy*, 25 (1): 1–25.

Fennell, M. (1999) *Overcoming Low Self-Esteem*. London: Robinson.

Flew, A. (1975) *Thinking About Thinking*. London: Fontana.

Frankl, V. E. (1985) *Man's Search for Meaning* (revised and updated). New York: Washington Square Press.

Free, M. L. (1999) *Cognitive Therapy in Groups*. Chichester: Wiley.

Freeman, A. and Dattilio, F. M. (1992) 'Cognitive therapy in the year 2000', in A. Freeman and F. M. Dattilio (eds), *Comprehensive Casebook of Cognitive Therapy*. New York: Plenum.

Freeman, A., Schrodt, G. R., Jr., Gilson, M. and Ludgate, J. W. (1993) 'Group cognitive therapy with inpatients', in J. H. Wright, M. E. Thase, A. T. Beck and J. W. Ludgate (eds), *Cognitive Therapy with Inpatients*. New York: Guilford.

Fuggle, P., Dunsmuir, S. and Curry, V. (2013) *CBT with Children, Young People and Families*. London: Sage.

Greenberger, D. and Padesky, C. A. (1995) *Mind Over Mood*. New York: Guilford.

Grieger, R. and Boyd, J. (1980) *Rational–Emotive Therapy: A Skills-Based Approach*. New York: Van Nostrand Reinhold.

Hanna, F. J. (2002) *Therapy with Difficult Clients*. Washington, DC: American Psychological Association.

Hauck, P. (1982) *How To Do What You Want To Do*. London: Sheldon.

Hayes, S., Strosahl, K. and Wilson, K. (2011) *Acceptance and Commitment Therapy: The Process and Practice of Mindful Change*, 2nd edn. New York: Guilford.

Irvine, W. B. (2009) *A Guide to the Good Life: The Ancient Art of Stoic Joy*. New York: Oxford University Press.

Irvine, W. B. (2013) *A Slap in the Face: Why Insults Hurt – and Why They Shouldn't*. New York: Oxford University Press.

James, I. A. (2001) 'Schema therapy: the next generation, but should it carry a health warning?', *Behavioural and Cognitive Psychotherapy*, 29 (4): 401–407.

James, I. A. (2010) *Cognitive Behavioural Therapy with Older People*. London: Jessica Kingsley.

Kazantzis, N., Deane, F. P., Ronan, K. R. and L'Abate, L. (eds) (2005) *Using Homework Assignments in Cognitive Behavior Therapy*. New York: Routledge.

Kirk, J. (1989) 'Cognitive-behavioural assessment', in K. Hawton, P. M. Salkovskis, J. Kirk and D. M. Clark (eds), *Cognitive Behaviour Therapy for Psychiatric Problems: A Practical Guide*. Oxford: Oxford University Press.

Kolakowski, L. (2008) *Why is There Something Rather Than Nothing? Questions from Great Philosophers*. London: Penguin.

Kroese, B. S., Dagnan, D. and Loumidis, K. (1997) *Cognitive Behaviour Therapy for People with Learning Disabilities*. London: Brunner-Routledge.

Kuehlwein, K. T. (2002) 'The cognitive treatment of depression', in G. Simos (ed.), *Cognitive Behaviour Therapy: A Guide for the Practising Clinician*. Hove: Brunner-Routledge.

Kuyken, W., Padesky, C. and Dudley, R. (2009) *Collaborative Case Conceptualization*. New York: Guilford.

Kwee, M. G. T. and Lazarus, A. A. (1986) 'Multimodal therapy: the cognitive-behavioural tradition and beyond', in W. Dryden and W. Golden (eds), *Cognitive-Behavioural Approaches to Psychotherapy*. London: Harper & Row.

Laidlaw, K., Thompson, L. W., Dick-Siskin, L. and Gallagher-Thompson, D. (2003) *Cognitive Behaviour Therapy with Older People*. Chichester: Wiley.

Lazarus, A. (1984) *In the Mind's Eye*. New York: Guilford.

Lazarus, A. and Fay, A. (1982) 'Resistance or rationalization? A cognitive-behavioral perspective', in P. Wachtel (ed.), *Resistance: Psychodynamic and Behavioral Approaches*. New York: Plenum.

Leahy, R. L. (2001) *Overcoming Resistance in Cognitive Therapy*. New York: Guilford.

Leahy, R. L. (2003) *Cognitive Therapy Techniques*. New York: Guilford.

Leahy, R. L. (2008) 'The therapeutic relationship in cognitive-behavioral therapy', *Behavioural and Cognitive Psychotherapy*, 36 (6): 769–77.

Leahy, R. L. (2010) *Beat the Blues Before They Beat You: How to Overcome Depression*. Carlsbad, CA: Hay House.

Leahy, R. L., Holland, S. J. and McGinn, L. K. (2012) *Treatment Plans and Interventions for Depression and Anxiety Disorders*, 2nd edn. New York: Guilford.

Ledley, D. R., Marx, B. P., and Heimberg, R. G. (2010) *Making Cognitive-Behavioral Therapy Work*, 2nd edn. New York: Guilford.

Linehan, M. (1993) *Cognitive-Behavioral Treatment of Borderline Personality Disorder*. New York: Guilford.

Mansell, W. and Taylor, J. (2012) 'What is CBT and what isn't CBT', in W. Dryden and R. Branch (eds), *The CBT Handbook*. London: Sage.

Marlatt, G. A. and Gordon, J. R. (eds) (1985) *Relapse Prevention: Maintenance Strategies in the Treatment of Addictive Behaviors*. New York: Guilford.

Martell, C. R., Dimidjian, S. and Herman-Dunn, R. (2010) *Behavioral Activation for Depression*. New York: Guilford.

McKay, M. and Fanning, P. (1991) *Prisoners of Belief*. Oakland, CA.: New Harbinger.

McKay, M., Davis, M. and Fanning, P. (2011) *Thoughts and Feelings: Taking Control of Your Moods and Your Life*, 4th edn. Oakland, CA: New Harbinger.

Mooney, K. A. and Padesky, C. A. (2000) 'Applying client creativity to recurrent problems: constructing possibilities and tolerating doubt', *Journal of Cognitive Psychotherapy*, 14 (2): 149–161.

Moorey, S. (1990) 'Cognitive therapy', in W. Dryden (ed.), *Individual Therapy: A Handbook*. Milton Keynes: Open University Press.

Morrison, A. (ed.) (2001) *A Casebook of Cognitive Therapy for Psychosis*. Hove: Brunner-Routledge.

Naugle, A. E. and Follette, W. C. (1998) 'A functional analysis of trauma symptoms', in V. M. Follette, J. I. Ruzek and F. R. Abueg (eds), *Cognitive-Behavioral Therapies for Trauma*. New York: Guilford.

Neenan, M. (2009) *Developing Resilience: A Cognitive-Behavioural Approach*. Hove: Routledge.

Neenan, M. and Dryden, W. (2000) *Essential Cognitive Therapy*. London: Whurr.

Neenan, M. and Dryden, W. (2002) *Cognitive Behaviour Therapy: An A– Z of Persuasive Arguments.* London: Whurr.

Neenan, M. and Dryden, W. (2011) *Cognitive Therapy in a Nutshell,* 2nd edn.. London: Sage.

Neenan, M. and Dryden, W. (2014) *Life Coaching: A Cognitive Behavioural Approach,* 2nd edn. Hove: Routledge.

Neenan, M. and Palmer, S. (1998) 'A cognitive-behavioural approach to tackling stress', *Counselling, the Journal of the British Association for Counselling,* 9 (4): 315–319.

Newman, C. F. (1989) 'Where's the evidence? A clinical tip', *International Cognitive Therapy Newsletter,* 5 (1): 4, 8.

Newman, C. F. (2000) 'Hypotheticals in cognitive psychotherapy: creative questions, novel answers, and therapeutic change', *Journal of Cognitive Psychotherapy,* 14 (2): 135–147.

Newman, C. F. (2013) *Core Competencies in Cognitive-Behavioral Therapy.* New York: Routledge.

Newman, C. F., Leahy, R. L., Beck, A. T., Reilly-Harrington, N. A. and Gyulai, L. (2002) *Bipolar Disorder: A Cognitive Therapy Approach.* Washington, DC: American Psychological Association.

Padesky, C. A. (1993a) 'Staff and patient education', in J. H. Wright, M. E. Thase, A. T. Beck and J. W. Ludgate (eds), *Cognitive Therapy with Inpatients.* New York: Guilford.

Padesky, C. A. (1993b) 'Socratic questioning: changing minds or guiding discovery?' A keynote address delivered at the European Congress of Behavioural and Cognitive Therapies, London, 24 September.

Padesky, C. A. (1994) 'Schema change processes in cognitive therapy', *Clinical Psychology and Psychotherapy,* 1 (5): 267–278.

Padesky, C. A. (1996) 'Developing cognitive therapist competency: teaching and supervision models', in P. M. Salkovskis (ed.), *Frontiers of Cognitive Therapy.* New York: Guilford.

Padesky, C. A. and Greenberger, D. (1995) *Clinician's Guide to Mind Over Mood.* New York: Guilford.

Persons, J. B. (1989) *Cognitive Therapy in Practice: A Case Formulation Approach*. New York: Norton.

Persons, J. B., Burns, D. D. and Perloff, J. M. (1988) 'Predictors of dropout and outcome in cognitive therapy for depression in a private practice setting', *Cognitive Therapy and Research*, 12 (6): 557–575.

Robertson, D. (2010) *The Philosophy of Cognitive-Behavioural Therapy (CBT): Stoic Philosophy as Rational and Cognitive Psychotherapy*. London: Karnac.

Safran, J. D. and Muran, J. C. (2000) *Negotiating the Therapeutic Alliance*. New York: Guilford.

Safran, J. D. and Segal, Z. V. (1990) *Interpersonal Process in Cognitive Therapy*. New York: Basic Books.

Salkovskis, P. M. (1991) 'The importance of behaviour in the maintenance of anxiety and panic: a cognitive account', *Behavioural Psychotherapy*, 19: 6–19.

Salkovskis, P. M. and Clark, D. M. (1991) 'Cognitive therapy for panic disorder', *Journal of Cognitive Psychotherapy*, 5 (3): 215–226.

Scott, M. J. (2009) *Simply Effective Cognitive Behaviour Therapy*. Hove: Routledge.

Segal, Z., Williams, M. and Teasdale, J. (2013) *Mindfulness-Based Cognitive Therapy for Depression*, 2nd edn. New York: Guilford.

Shafran, R., Brosan, L., and Cooper, P. (eds) (2013) *The Complete CBT Guide for Anxiety*. London: Robinson.

Stallard, P. (2002) *Think Good–Feel Good: A Cognitive Behaviour Therapy Workbook for Children and Young People*. Chichester: Wiley.

Taylor, S. (2006) *Clinician's Guide to PTSD: A Cognitive-Behavioral Approach*. New York: Guilford.

Tinch, C. S. and Friedberg, R. D. (1996) 'The schema identification worksheet: a guide for clients and clinicians', *International Cognitive Therapy Newsletter*, 10 (4): 1–4.

Tompkins, M. A. (2004) *Using Homework in Psychotherapy*. New York: Guilford.

Twohig, M., Woidneck, M. and Crosby, J. (2013) 'Newer generations of CBT for anxiety disorders', in G. Simos and S. Hofmann (eds) *CBT for Anxiety Disorders: A Practitioner Book*. Chichester: Wiley-Blackwell.

Walen, S. R., DiGiuseppe, R. and Dryden, W. (1992) *A Practitioner's Guide to Rational–Emotive Therapy*, 2nd edn. New York: Oxford University Press.

Warburton, N. (2007) *Thinking from A to Z*, 3rd edn. London: Routledge.

Weishaar, M. E. (1993) *Aaron T. Beck*. London: Sage.

Weishaar, M. E. (1996) 'Developments in cognitive therapy', in W. Dryden (ed.), *Developments in Psychotherapy: Historical Perspectives*. London: Sage.

Weishaar, M. E. and Beck, A. T. (1986) 'Cognitive therapy', in W. Dryden and W. Golden (eds), *Cognitive-Behavioural Approaches to Psychotherapy*. London: Harper & Row.

Wells, A. (1997) *Cognitive Therapy of Anxiety Disorders*. Chichester: Wiley.

Westbrook, D., Kennerley, H. and Kirk, J. (2011) *An Introduction to Cognitive Behaviour Therapy*, 2nd edn. London: Sage.

White, C. A. (2001) *Cognitive Behaviour Therapy for Chronic Medical Problems*. Chichester: Wiley.

Wills, F. (2012) 'Assessment and formulation in CBT', in W. Dryden and R. Branch (eds), *The CBT Handbook*. London: Sage.

Wills, F. and Sanders, D. (1997) *Cognitive Therapy: Transforming the Image*. London: Sage.

Willson, R. and Veale, D. (2009) *Overcoming Health Anxiety*. London: Robinson.

Young, J., Klosko, J. and Weishaar, M. (2003) *Schema Therapy: A Practitioner's Guide*. New York: Guilford.